Dedicated to the hundreds of thousands of men and women who have chosen to grow through their divorce and to the thousands more who have helped them rebuild their lives!

Special thanks to Robert Hawkins, Sr., founder of Harvest House Publishers. Without his wisdom, encouragement, and guidance, the dream of this book would never have become a reality.

Introduction

It has been many years since a small group of men and women met in my first divorce-recovery workshop in Garden Grove, California. In the hundreds of workshops I have conducted since, I have discovered that only the faces change. The needs remain the same.

Divorce is still one of the most painful and emotionally draining experiences that a human being can have. It results in the death of a marriage but does not have the finality of physical death. The vestiges of a former way of life remain to remind and overshadow a present existence. It is a hurt that goes deep and is accompanied by the doubt that it will ever heal.

In a society that has a pill or a prescription for almost any human ill, very little is being done to help the person struggling through the hurricane of divorce. Even though there are thousands of divorce support groups across America, many hurting men and women find themselves aching and alone when divorce shatters their dreams and tears apart their families.

This book comes from firsthand experience of being a national pioneer in the field of divorce recovery and working hand in hand with many thousands of people over the years. I have struggled with them, listened to their stories, shared boxes of Kleenex, and tried to say with hope and optimism, "You have a choice. You can either go through divorce or you can grow through divorce!"

Applying the principles found in this book, beginning with the ten steps on the next page, will help ease some of the pain caused by divorce and raise the hope of a new beginning for you.

Jim Smoke

How to Survive a Divorce

Ten things to do when you feel a
divorce is inevitable

_____

1. When the reality of divorce hits you, stop long enough to commit your entire situation to God through prayer, and ask Him to provide you with help, guidance, and emotional support.
2. Call your best friends and ask them for their prayers and emotional support.
3. Stay in touch with your feelings and share them with people you can trust.
4. Don't spiritualize your situation. You may have to live out a bad decision that someone else has made.
5. Don't panic! Remember, no matter what happens, God is still in charge.
6. Contact an attorney to find out about your legal grounds.
7. Make a list of all your fears. Then make a list of all your resources.
8. Pull as many members of your family around you as you can. Ask them for their love and support.
9. Seek out a divorce support group in your community. These are often held in churches and community colleges. Buy a copy of *Growing Through Divorce* and read it many times.
10. Remember, healing takes time. There is no quick fix for a divorce.

Contents

ONE

Is This Really Happening to Me?

"Divorce is not an event. It is a process. You grow through that process a minute, an hour, a day, a week at a time."

Shocked! Angry! Dazed! Bitter! Empty! Cheated! Rejected! These, along with an assortment of other feelings, probably describe how many people feel when they separate from a marriage that began with optimism, happiness, and hope. A terrible thing that somehow always happened to other people has happened to you. In many instances, there is little preparation for the chaos that you are thrown into both emotionally and physically. Many things that were once taken in stride now become major hazards in daily life. You are in "divorce country"! You never planned to be here but you are. It's a strange place with different rules, regulations, and road signs. You want it all to change and go away. But it won't!

Shock—Stage One

The first emotional state that many people go through in a divorce is shock. Shock is a reaction to the impact that this is really happening to me—not some statistic out there in society, but me.

In a state of shock, people react in many different ways. Some retreat within themselves, trying to block out all thoughts of what is happening. They deny the divorce mentally and refuse to talk about it with anyone. They withdraw from friends and social contacts. They may move or change jobs. Retreating sometimes turns into running.

Inward feelings may run the gamut from personal feelings of guilt and failure to the transference of those feelings totally to the other person.

People who go inward in a divorce tend to reject positive help and acceptance from others. Growth in a divorce begins with the admission that this is really happening to me. The first step in dealing with any situation is admitting the situation exists. Denying the divorce will not make it go away. Hiding it from family and friends will not resolve it.

Many people experiencing divorce have shared that enough people have isolated them without them having to impose an inward isolation upon themselves. There is a time, however, to evaluate, think through, and reflect upon what is happening to you. This constructive retreat generally happens after the shock state has passed.

In the shock state, other people tend to go outside themselves. This is prompted by the need to tell all and to tell everyone. Acceptance of the situation is fended off by the constant replay of all the details, feelings, and facts of the divorce. Any ear that will listen becomes a target for the talker.

For the outward person, a frantic social pace often keeps the reality of the situation at arm's length. Coming, going, and doing become all-important. If you are too busy to think, you cannot be hurt by your thoughts. But realities have a way of catching up with you, and facing them today will set tomorrow free.

In the shock stage, both the inward and the outward person slowly come to an acceptance of the fact that a relationship that once was vital, important, and real has died.

What About Hope?

Some people prolong the shock stage by desperately clinging to hope. They live on the hope that they can get back together again and that things will work out to a happy ending. They come to professional counselors with hope in their hearts. They look to God and ministers for miracles. They talk to friends and relatives and ask for help and hope. They often talk to the departed mate about reunion. Many refuse to let hope die and enter into a holding pattern that often lasts for years.

Without hope and optimism, life in general would be as dry as dust. But hope has to be coupled with realism. Realism looks at a situation as it exists, not as you would like it to exist. Realism evaluates a situation honestly based on past and present experience. Here are several questions that will help you sort out hope and reality.

1. *Do both parties really want the marriage?*

If a marriage is in trouble and both parties really want the marriage to succeed, there is a high degree of realistic hope providing they will accept professional help. If one party does not really want the marriage, it will not matter how strongly the other party wants it. Many people have no choice in the matter. If the other person has made the decision and leaves, you are reduced to the decision of waiting and hoping for their return or filing for a divorce.

It is always difficult to live out a bad decision that is made by someone else. I believe that you do all that you possibly can to save a marriage before you accept the decision to divorce.

Just remember, it takes two people working at reconciliation if a marriage is to be saved.

2. Will both parties accept professional help in reconciliation for as long as is necessary?

One of the questions I frequently ask divorced persons is whether or not they went for help when their marriage was deteriorating. Frequently they reply that they wanted and went for help but the other party felt they did not need it or it was not their problem to resolve. Counselors do not work one-party miracles in marriage very often. It takes two people working on the problem. The battle is already lost if only one person assumes responsibility. Many couples start counseling together with good intentions only to have one of them quit after a couple of sessions or take a dislike to the counselor at being probed and questioned. Too many people expect a session or two to solve what many years might have created. If one person refuses help, your chances are minimal that you will get your marriage back together.

3. Has a third party become involved with either mate?

The breakup of a marriage may be caused by internal strife within the marriage or by a third-party relationship being formed outside of the marriage. Since we do not have time to argue cause and effect here, we simply submit from experience that a third-party involvement usually brings the marriage to its end. Some partners will wait, forgive, endure, and try to forget. But the law of averages is pretty high that the third-party involvement will end the marriage.

About 75 percent of all divorces are caused by affairs. The remaining 25 percent happen when a person decides they can no longer live with things like alcoholism, drugs, addictions, and dysfunctional behaviors—and when in spite of their efforts, the person with the problem refuses all help.

4. *What have I learned from my past experiences that will shed light on my present situation?*

Experience is, for all of us, a good teacher. We learn by living and by experiencing. We can all look into our well of experience and draw from it. Hopefully, you will not have to marry many times in order to learn from experience. Many marriages contain elements that were out of control long before the marriage was a reality. But many people would rather face hope than reality, and they gamble that things will be different this time. Learn from your past!

Few people make dramatic changes in their life and lifestyle without some kind of outside help, whether from God or a professional. Just hoping a marriage will come back together by itself is like wishing on a chicken bone. Each person must evaluate whether the relationship has died or whether there is enough life to hold out some hope.

Adjustment—Stage Two

As the shock stage of a divorce begins to wear away, a process of adjustment—stage two—begins to take place. Adjustment means you begin to deal with the reality that this has really happened to you. Shock is accepting the facts of divorce; adjustment is doing something about it.

There is a period of time in most divorces that is similar to that experienced at the loss of a mate through death. It is a time of grief, mourning, or sorrow over a relationship that is lost. Just as people accept shock in different ways, people also accept mourning in different ways. They can go inward or outward.

Positive Mourning

Positive mourning is the experience of remembering the good, happy, fun-filled memories of your marriage and forgetting the bad memories. It's being glad you had the good times and wishing you still had them. It's being sorry that they are gone now and knowing that there is still much happiness left for you in life. Happiness is not born in marriage and killed in divorce. Positive mourning says I have the human right to feel loss, grief, and sorrow. It says I hurt and for now there is an empty space in my life. I can cry because they are positive tears.

Negative Mourning

Negative mourning is the experience of swimming in a sea of self-pity. It usually starts with the assumption that the marriage dissolution was all my fault or all his or her fault. Once this idea is projected, the person locks himself into a mental room and throws the key away. He defies others to break down the door and release him from his self-imposed misery. Life has dealt him a bad hand and his relief comes from telling everyone his miseries. Feeling sorry for yourself should be limited to a five-second experience about once a week. It is self-defeating and often leads into deep mental depression. If you obtained all the pity that you wanted from other people, what would you have? A warehouse full of "I'm so sorrys"!

Assembling the Pieces

Jigsaw puzzle fans go about their hobby in an interesting way. They dump all the pieces of the puzzle on a table, turn them all right side up, then slowly begin putting them together.

Sometimes they leave the puzzle for a time and return to work on it later. The project methodically goes on until the last piece is in place. The picture is completed—success is attained.

Life is a daily process of putting the pieces of a puzzle together. We do a little each day, and slowly the picture takes shape. In a divorce, the pieces to the puzzle get tossed all over the house, and some are even lost for a while. Some get in the wrong place and don't fit too well. Persistence, perseverance, and patience help us keep working on the puzzle. Slowly the pieces come together. In the adjustment stage, pieces to the puzzle are being identified, turned right side up, and slowly put into place. Each chapter in this book will help you put some of the pieces of the divorce puzzle together. Adjustment sometimes means we can't have things exactly as we want them. We adjust to the situation as it is, knowing that it will change.

Adjustment is also a time of transition. It is passing from one lifestyle (married) to another lifestyle (single). Patterns of living that were firmly established in marriage have now been disrupted and the new pattern has not yet been fully devel oped. Adjustment is often marked by restlessness, disorganiza-tion, and extreme highs and lows in feelings. Loneliness creeps in and out. And the burden of being a single parent can settle like an unyielding yoke upon your shoulders.

Adjustment sometimes means that you have to make very important decisions for yourself, family, and future while you are at your emotional worst. The temptation is often to throw all the pieces of your puzzle into the air and hope that they will fall together when they land.

Take the time to sort the pieces out, place them right side up, and see if they fit together. Getting away from the puzzle for a while often helps you get the pieces into better perspective when you return.

The period of adjustment may take many months. Time is a healer and cannot be hurried. Many people in post-divorce adjustment want to hurry the hurts away and experience instant new health. Divorce recovery takes time.

After many years of working in the divorce-recovery field, I have discovered that it takes most men and women from two to three years to recover from a divorce.

Growth—Stage Three

When was the last time you checked to see if the grass outside your house was still growing? That's silly. No one checks their grass. You just wait a week, it grows, you cut it, wait another week, and it's time to cut it again. The point is that your grass grows even though you can't see it growing. Growth in human lives works the same way. You grow a little each day even if you can't see it or feel it. Good growth happens when conditions are right, both in lawns and in lives. Good growth begins when a person says, "I want to grow and learn from my experiences."

In a recent conversation, I asked a person how they were doing. The response was "Not too good," followed by, "I'm going through a divorce."

The response was typical of most people. We are all going through different things each day. The difference is that you have a choice whether you will simply go through divorce or grow through it.

Growing through a divorce means you say, "I will learn all I can learn from this experience, and I will be a stronger and better person because of this learning experience."

If anyone had come to you prior to your divorce and asked what you knew about divorce, you probably would have replied, "Not very much." You possibly could have added that you had known people who had divorced, but you had little personal experience with the problem until now.

Growing is learning all you can about a given situation or thing. Divorce can be either a negative, self-defeating experience in your life or a positive, growth-producing experience. It depends on what you are willing to learn from it and how you put what you have learned into practice.

Let me share nine "growing through divorce" steps with you.

1. Realize that time is a healer and you must walk through that process one day at a time. No one can walk through it for you. No one else will have your exact feelings and experiences. Some days the growth time will be an hour or maybe even half of a day. But you will grow only as you walk through the process.

2. Come to grips with yourself. You can't deny your existence no matter how frustrated, lonely, guilty, angry, or desperate you may feel.

3. Set aside time for reflection, meditation, reading, thinking, and personal growth. There are many situations around you that you will be powerless to change. But you can always work on changing yourself. Allow yourself some time to do this.

4. Get with healthy people who are struggling but growing. There is only minimal comfort in hearing other people's divorce stories while you are going through yours. At first it may be a help, but it soon becomes a bore. Healthy people are those who let the past die and who live and grow in the present.

Many churches and community colleges today offer weekly divorce support groups. Make a few phone calls and see if there is one near you.

5. Seek professional counseling or therapy if you feel you need it. Asking for help is a sign of strength, not weakness.

Many counseling centers offer divorce-recovery workshops that can be invaluable in helping you gain insight into your situation.

6. Accept the fact that you are divorced (or divorcing) and now single. Many divorced people still feel married. A lady summed up her feelings one day by saying that she was not single but merely between marriages. If you are divorced, you are single.

7. Watch out for relational rescue attempts. When we are in pain, we are emotionally vulnerable to anyone with an outstretched hand and kind word. Some people prey on hurting people. Be on your guard.

8. Put the past in the past and live in the present.

9. Commit your new way to God, begin new things, and seek the help and relationships you need to begin again.

None of these growth-producing steps are easy. You have to begin where you are, even if you feel you are fresh out of new beginnings.

Society has a way of looking at divorce and spelling it F-A-I-L-U-R-E. Even though it is widely accepted as a way of life in our world, it still carries its brand on people's lives. We somehow will give people the right to fail in business, in school, in careers, but not in marriage. The contemporary church, in particular, has looked upon divorce as the unforgivable sin while preaching that man is not perfect, must live with his humanity, and has the freedom to fail. A divorced person has enough of a struggle living with his own weight of judgment without having that weight added to by others. Someone asked me recently who suffered the most in a divorce: a man, a woman, or the children. My response was "People!"

Four Goals for Good Growth

Some wise person once said, "Shoot at nothing, and that is what you will hit." It is hard to set goals and work at them when you are in the chaos of divorce. But without those goals, you will never hit the target of growth. Here are four simple ones that you can work on each week.

1. Look at your divorce-recovery process as a healing experience. You are recovering from the surgery of loss. All healing takes time. Your goal is to give yourself time to heal. Remember, two to three years!

2. Begin to develop a new support system that will give you a sense of belonging and identity for your time of transition. One of the painful things in divorce is that you often lose most of your married friends. Your goal is to slowly build a new support system for your life.

3. Give yourself time for emotional drainage. We do one of two things with our emotions. We express them or repress them. Only by expressing them do we find a sense of relief and healing. There will always be a few people who will let you turn on your emotional tap and spill its contents. Putting on a happy face when you have a sad heart only denies your feelings. Remember, the Bible says there is a season for everything.

4. Be willing to integrate your divorce experience with that of other people in the form of caring, sharing, contrasting, and supporting. Even when you are at the bottom of the well humanly, you can find something to give to another hurting person. They in turn will give to you.

---

*Always remember, in a divorce you get
custody of yourself!*

TWO

Letting Go

---

*"I can only live in the present
if I let go of the past."*

One of the earliest hurdles to be faced in a divorce is the struggle of letting go of the many things that were a part of the marriage experience. Divorce brings a vast number of changes into the lives of those involved. One person described it recently as "the catapult from a four-bedroom house in suburbia to an apartment in exile." Few people can go through a divorce with their old life and lifestyle remaining intact.

There are a few adventuresome persons who welcome changes in life, but most of us are somewhat threatened by changes and the fear of the unknown. Divorce forces people to change. Change involves letting go of old things and accepting new things.

Every life is maintained by various support systems. We grow and depend upon mental, social, physical, and spiritual structures for our support. When any of these structures is weakened, we become confused, disoriented, frustrated, insecure, or uncertain. Divorce introduces numerous changes in each of these four areas.

Mental

The mental area is how we utilize our mind and how our mind reacts to what is going on around us. We develop attitudes in our mind toward our former spouse, our children, our relatives, and our friends.

The state of marriage in these four supporting groups of people gives us one set of attitudes. The state of divorce usually reverses our attitudes toward these people as well as their attitudes toward us. Former-spouse attitudes can go from love to hate overnight. The attitudes of children can vary from "the divorce is all your fault" to "the divorce is all my fault." Relatives can line up on either spouse's team. Friends can choose their objectivity and choose sides or disappear completely.

Coping on the mental level with our own feelings and attitudes and with the feelings and attitudes of other people can become an awesome burden. Learning to "let go" in this area means coming to the realization and recognition that I am responsible for my attitudes and feelings but not for the attitudes and feelings of others. There will be changes in other people's response to me that I can do very little about. Things will not remain as they were prior to the divorce. People will not remain as they were, even though you wish they would. Divorce sets in motion the wheels of change in attitudes and relationships. Accepting and understanding this will help you live in the present rather than in the past. First attitudes and reactions to a divorce are often not permanent ones. But divorce does affect other people around you, and they have a right to their own responses and attitudes.

Social

The social world of a person involves job/career, school/ education, church/religion, community interaction, and lifestyle. As human beings, we need to interact with other human beings. We form ties and relationships as we weave the fabric of our lifestyle about us. A divorce not only draws attitudes and reactions from those in our personal world, but it also calls for a response from those in our various social worlds.

Society is generally constructed for couples, pairs, twos. The ultimate of that coupling is marriage. When people divorce, those in these social worlds respond by asking how this will affect *them*, more than how this will affect the people divorcing. The "what people think" syndrome takes over, judgments are made, and verdicts are rendered. The social world often lets go of the divorcing person before the divorcing person has the chance to adjust or change social involvements. A job can be lost and a career ended. School life and peer-teacher misunderstanding can be devastating to children. (Attitudes of the church and organized religious life will be examined under the spiritual area.) Involvements with various community agencies, clubs, and organizations are often terminated. "I was married—I now am single" prompts a sudden shift in lifestyle from married friends to single friends. This often occurs after building only married friendships for 20 or more years.

Letting go in the social realm means I will have to face some changes, discriminations, and reactions in this area. I cannot continue as before. But I will struggle and fight to maintain the involvements I want, and I will work hard at building new and rewarding social involvements.

Physical

"One of the worst things about a divorce is coming home at the end of a day to an apartment or house and not having the physical presence of another adult to share your joys and sorrows with." This response is typical of the many I hear from formerly married persons who face the loss of a mate. Divorce brings about the loss of love, but it also brings the removal of the physical presence of the other partner from the home. Not having someone there to talk things over with—no one to laugh with and to cry with—can be the most awesome burden to the divorced person. Loneliness creates a hostile environment in which fears are heightened. All divorced persons must face the reality that they stand as one, not two. Many people stay in a marriage long after the love has gone just so they will not physically be alone.

Letting go in the physical area means slowly accepting the reality that the other person is not there any longer and will never be there again. Accepting this reality means accepting the hurt of being alone. But being alone right now is not a life sentence imposed as a penalty for your divorce.

The physical area may also involve the loss of a home environment. Someone has said that a house is where you live; a home is what people make that house into. I resent the use of the term "a broken home" to describe a divorce. A broken home seems to convey to me the idea that it is permanently destroyed and the people who have lived there are beyond repair. If you allow a divorce to give you "a broken home," it will. A better attitude and response would be to acknowledge that your home environment was dented, dinged, bent, or bruised. These terms admit damage but do not preclude repair.

In the world of automobile accidents, "totaled" means your car is not worth fixing. A divorce may make you feel "totaled" and beyond repair in all areas, but don't believe it! Your life may not be the shiny new model it was at the marriage altar, but the dents and scratches that a divorce has made in it can be repaired with your help, the help of other people, and the help of God.

Spiritual

A divorce can drive you away from God or drive you to God. In my personal counseling, many people tell me that their divorce has caused them to reexamine their relationship to God. They have realigned their priorities and commitments to God and the church. The church, however, does not always make it easy on the divorced person to affirm faith and experience forgiveness.

Many people who experience divorce while involved in church and religious life are asked to move their membership and families elsewhere. Others are removed from future leadership roles in the life of the church and are imprisoned in the pews as a permanent penance for their misdeeds.

Spiritual isolation is often experienced by the religious person who goes through a divorce, while the nonreligious person is attracted to the church that seeks to understand, have empathy, and show forgiveness. There are too few churches, however, that welcome the formerly married.

Letting go in the spiritual area means giving your divorce situation over to God and letting Him weigh it, judge it, and balance it. It means knowing the difference between God's forgiveness and other people's lack of forgiveness. It means understanding that God is the author of new beginnings.

A New Identity

Letting go of old things means replacing them with new things. New things have to be acknowledged and accepted on the mental level before they can be lived out on the physical, social, and spiritual levels.

Many divorced persons tell me that they feel married and act married, but live single. Growth in divorce is accepting its realities. In a divorce workshop that I teach, we ask people to repeat out loud the following sentences: "I am divorced. I am single. I am OK."

At first, it is mumbled rather softly. After a couple of times, it is said more firmly. Why do we do this? Because many people feel one way but have to live another. We try to help them get reality, feelings, and living together. It starts by making a positive mental statement of who you are. When a person loses their identity, they are not sure who they are. In order to be healthy and growing, they must have an identity again. And they must accept what they are whether they like it or not.

Keys to Accepting a New Identity

1. Don't keep living in the role of the old identity. The longer you do this, the longer you will block the potential for new growth. You are not married, so don't play the role. You are single, and you must slowly discover what this new role is like and how to enact it.

2. Create "new experiences in living" for yourself. It's easy to live and relive your old experiences. Creating new experiences in living will help you become an adventurer in the present rather than a tenant of the past.

3. Don't let other people superimpose an identity upon you. It's sometimes easier to become what other people want us to be rather than what we really want to be. Form your own identity. You are you, not what someone else is or thinks you are.

4. Learn all you can about your new identity and how to live it. Learn about being single, being a single parent, being a

weekend parent, being alone, being resourceful, being independent, being a new person.

5. Realize that you are a unique, unrepeatable miracle of God. Developing a relationship with God gives foundation to your new identity.

6. Know that you have the freedom to fail. We live with our humanity, and that humanity causes us to make mistakes. Take risks and learn from your failures.

How Long Does It Take?

We all live by the clock. We alternately try to save time and waste time. Many divorced persons want to know how long it will take to get over their divorce and the many hurts experienced in it. How long will it be before I feel good, whole, and together again? How long does it take to fall in love? How long does it take to fall out of love?

It all takes time! For some people a short amount, for others a long time. Some heal quickly and forget easily. Other people heal slowly and never forget. Decide for yourself right now that you will take all the time you need to let go of old things and build new things—that you will not become impatient but will understand that this is a new and growing experience for you.

Remember, two to three years is a good measuring stick.

Let go of the past. There's no future in it!

Personal Growth and Discussion Questions

1. How did the following support people react to your divorce?
   former spouse
   children
   relatives
   friends

2. What effect has your divorce had upon the social areas of your life?

3. How do you handle the absence of a "physical presence" in your home?

4. What effect did your divorce have in the spiritual areas of your life?

5. What plan do you have for developing a new identity for yourself?

6. My personal goal for this week is

THREE

Getting the Former Spouse in Focus

"I loved you, I hate you,
I'll get you."

How can the feelings for a former spouse go so rapidly from love to hate to revenge?"

I've been asked that question many times by many people who are caught at the feeling level in their divorce. Conditions and situations can cause the feelings in a person to go from one extreme to another in the short space of seconds or the lengthened span of years.

Divorce, unlike death, does not fully remove the former spouse from daily existence. Former spouses hover about the edges of a marriage dissolution and frequently wreak havoc with the other mate's life. Different reactions of the involved parties in a divorce often relate directly to the causes that led to the divorce.

There are eight basic causes of divorce that seem to appear with the most frequency.

1. *The "Victim" Divorce*

The victim divorce is a setting where one mate leaves the home for another person. It may be a secretary, close friend, old friend, new friend, etc. The results are the same. One person wants the divorce while the other person does not. The mate left behind may suffer feelings of rejection, guilt, worthlessness, and despair that can soon turn into anger and revenge. Hostility toward the former spouse is usually the highest in the victim divorce.

2. The "Problem" Divorce

A problem divorce usually stems from the problem or problems your mate had prior to your marriage or developed after your marriage began. The most common problems today involve all forms of addictions, dysfunctions from family background, mid-life crisis personality changes, homosexuality, and career and vocational changes. Solutions can be found to most problems if both partners commit to finding the answer. Tragically, many men and women with problems deny they have them, and the hope for help and resolution never gets grounded in the reality of recovery. Spousal feelings in this kind of divorce run from sympathy for the former spouse to anger and regret that one may have given up so many years hoping for an answer to the problem. The person with the "problem" can feel angry and hostile at being left and try all sorts of knee-jerk recovery in order to get the former spouse back. Always remember, recovery takes time!

3. The "Little Boy, Little Girl" Divorce

This divorce is prompted by the fact that one mate or the other decides that they don't want the responsibility of being husband or wife, or mother or father. They decide that they want to spend their time with the "boys" or the "girls" and play with the kind of toys they played with before marriage. The only difference is the price of the toys. Personal immaturity and the unwillingness to assume responsibility brings on the divorce. Feelings here are centered in rejection.

4. *The "I Was Conned" Divorce*

In simplest terms, this means that one mate or the other did not get what they thought they were getting in the marriage. The inability of one person to be honest with the other often leads to disillusionment and divorce later. This kind of divorce usually leads to a defensiveness toward the former spouse and a general distrust of the opposite sex.

5. *The "Shotgun" Divorce*

Most people have heard of the shotgun wedding. It is usually initiated by the fact that the bride-to-be is pregnant and family, friends, and community feel the honorable way to resolve the problem is by marriage. In many instances, shotgun weddings bring about shotgun divorces. Shotgun marriages involve living under the gun for both parties, and marriage by coercion doesn't always work too well. Feelings for the former spouse in this divorce setting run from pity to rejection.

6. *The "Mid-life Crisis" or "Menopause" Divorce*

We know that women go through menopause, but there is a growing belief in some medical circles that men go through some kind of state similar to menopause in women. In both sexes, dramatic changes in personality and behavior can cause one mate or the other to leave the marriage. Attitudes toward the former spouse after this kind of divorce are centered in lack of understanding and a general confusion as to what really happened. Because this can happen after many years of marriage, a deep hurt and bitterness is coupled to an abandoned feeling.

There has been a dramatic increase in the number of long-term marriages ending. Half of the many divorce-recovery classes across the country contain men and women who have been married 25 to 45 years. What this really means is that Grandma and Grandpa are now getting divorced.

7. *The "No Fault" Divorce*

A few years ago, divorcing parties had to state the causes for the divorce. Charges and countercharges were filed. Witnesses were brought forth to testify to the truth or lack of it. With the changing divorce laws in many states, there is no cause or reason needed. No one is held at fault. Often, two people just decide that they have had it with each other. They want to go their separate ways. Feelings in this kind of divorce are usually very neutral. The people involved feel it just didn't work out and it wasn't anyone's fault.

8. *The "Rat Race" Divorce*

The sign said it all: "The Rat Race Is Over, the Rats Won!" A more updated version might be "The Rat Race Is Not Over, But It Caused My Divorce!" We live in the world of "husband and wife both work" communities. The years of stress and strain that can build up in that kind of environment are overwhelming. Closeness and intimacy are lost to the increasing pressure of making all the payments. Somewhere in the middle, the children fight for their own survival. In the end, everyone runs out of emotional gas and the family sputters into divorce country.

Getting along with a former spouse when feelings and hurt levels are running high demands a great deal of patience and understanding. If no children are involved in the divorce or if the children are grown, married, and out of the home, there is only minimal need for ongoing personal contact or confrontation. Where children are involved, the reminders of the heartaches and hurts are highly visible. In the immediate post-divorce days, the conflict level between spouses is generally highest. As time passes and new interests and relationships are formed, the conflict level subsides. Visitations, support payments, vacations, and daily problems seem to fall into an acceptable pattern of existence. The hurts remain but the aggravation level seems to go down. Growth in dealing with a former spouse takes place when your feelings of hostility, hatred, and revenge mellow first to feelings of guilt and being sorry for yourself and your former spouse and finally to feelings of indifference and acceptance. This process of time and working through your feelings may take several years. There is no instant cure, although many search for it. Feelings are healed in time. Growth in new areas will modify your feelings.

People who experience divorce will often find that their feelings for the former mate will vary from day to day. When they don't see the person, they may find themselves wanting a reunion. When they do see the person, they may experience disgust, hatred, and hurt. It is easy to live in the dream world of what a person was rather than what a person is. Sometimes the inability to start a new life will send a person back to the old mate. Fear of the new in this instance can become greater than the fear of the old.

Ongoing Issues with a Former Spouse

There are 11 basic issues that never quite seem to get resolved when you take up residency in divorce country. They can start the minute that a divorce is announced and continue through the years until you finally depart planet Earth. They are listed here so that you can be aware of them and develop a plan to face them down whenever they hit you.

1. *Mixed Feelings.* One day you feel you still love your former spouse, the next day you hate and want to hurt him or her.

2. *Physically seeing or not seeing your former spouse.* There will be days when you never want to see the person again and other days when you will do everything to sneak a peek at your former spouse from afar.

3. *Talking to or not talking to your former spouse.* Some persons can talk amicably anytime with a former spouse while others find audible expression impossible. The great temptation is to use the telephone just to hear their voice or tell them how terrible you think they are.

4. *Financial support versus no financial support.* Most former spouse battles are fought in the financial arena. It is no secret that the woman's financial base erodes more than the man's after divorce. Millions of dollars annually are owed in back child-support payments. New laws are now attacking that problem.

5. *Sees or does not see the children.* There are many single parents who give love and time to their children. There are many who do not. You cannot make a parent stay connected with a child if the adult chooses otherwise. Tragically, children bear the brunt of this loss and can be haunted by rejection for years to come.

6. *Replaced or not replaced.* It is tough to face the fact that someone else is now taking the place you once filled in your former spouse's life. There is often a temptation to go find someone so that you won't feel left out in the world of meaningful relationships.

7. *One lifestyle improves, one worsens.* It is tough to be counting your pennies each month while your former spouse

is leasing a new luxury car or your former wife's new boyfriend has moved her into a mansion on the hill while you reside in a studio apartment by the train tracks.

8. *Good memories versus bad memories.* The bad memories of divorce can rob you of good past memories you had with a former spouse. Learn to file the good and bad memories and realize that life gives you both as collectibles on your journey. Oh, and keep the family photograph albums and videos. There will be a day you can look at them again without crying.

9. *Who's for me, who's for him or her?* Most people tend to take sides. Many who say they don't and won't still do. They just don't express their feelings verbally. Don't make people choose teams after your divorce. Work at keeping the friends you want and let the rest go.

10. *Get out of the combat zone.* Staying in protracted battles with your former spouse can sap the energy you need to rebuild your life. Some things are not worth fighting over. It only takes one to stop the war. You!

11. *Stop playing the blame game.* The very favorite, all-time former spouse after-dinner game is the blame game. Remember, blaming is basically a way of shifting responsibility and maintaining power over your former spouse.

You may want to add some issues of your own to this list. Part of the solution is knowing what the problems are. The following growth guidelines will help you resolve some of the former spouse issues.

Growth Guidelines in Getting the Former Spouse in Focus

1. *Take the detachment a day at a time.* One of the soundest principles I know in working your way through a divorce is to simply take things a day at a time. Wishing tomorrow were

here will not make today go away. Worrying about the future will not help you live in the present. Decide to live each day as it comes. Emotional healing can be slower than any physical healing you have ever experienced. Get used to living in the "now." Problems are resolved one day at a time. Plans are made one day at a time. Most people experiencing divorce feel that they are just not going to make it. They feel this way because they spend most of their mental energies racing backward into the past or forward into the future.

When the future is uncertain, there is a great tendency to simply worry about it. Worry never changes anything. The apostle Paul shared some wise words on worry with an early group of Christians. He said, "Be anxious for nothing, but in everything by prayer and supplication with thanksgiving, let your requests be made known to God. And the peace of God, which surpasses all comprehension, shall guard your hearts and your minds in Christ Jesus" (Philippians 4:6,7). You only need strength for today. As you test your strength on each day, you will build a reservoir for all your tomorrows.

Losing a person from your life who was once so important and integral to your existence is extremely hard. In many marriages, people's identities are so closely interwoven that they feel they cease to exist without the other person. You do exist. You are alive. You will make it through today!

2. *Try to make the break as clean as possible.* Many divorced persons don't know how to "quit their marriage." They keep struggling to free themselves from the former spouse while secretly wanting to hold on. Some former mates use every opportunity to see the other person and then regret it after having done so. They might keep hoping that the other person has changed or that their memory of the bad things will go away. Many departed mates return at will to their former home for meals, evenings, baby-sitting, gardening, repairs, or

nostalgia. Sometimes at "visiting dinner guest" level, former mates find themselves quite compatible and friendly. Remember that visiting together is vastly different from living together. Three months of separation is seldom able to heal 20 years of hurts and problems.

In most instances, physical separation should initiate a clean break between former mates. A lingering post-divorce attachment will prohibit the establishing of a new identity and positive growth.

Visitation rights where children are involved should be established and followed. Maintenance of the home should be planned and adhered to. The paying of support payments should not be used as an admission ticket to the former home.

Seeing a former mate usually does very little for the personal ego. It only reminds an individual of the past and the things he or she no longer has. It doesn't change anything. The sooner you begin building a new life for yourself, the happier you will be.

I have known people who decide to divorce and still live in the same house for extended periods of time. I have known others who separate but still maintain a dating relationship. These and other continuing relationships after a divorce has been decided upon will only prohibit you from experiencing a new beginning and a new sense of personal self-worth.

3. *Quit accepting responsibility for the former spouse.* Many of us feel responsible in life for things that we can't control. A vital part of mature growth is learning to accept responsibility for yourself, as we state in chapter 4. A further part of that maturity is to let other people accept responsibility for themselves. Many former mates feel an ongoing responsibility for their former partner. They may wonder if the "ex" can make it alone, if he or she will commit suicide, go hungry, or have a nervous breakdown. All of these concerns and many others

may be felt for the former mate. Attempts to mother or father a former spouse often follow hard on the heels of an emotion-wrenching divorce.

Few people learn to stand alone and discover their own resources until they have to. Children will let their parents do all the work and worry for as long as they can. Some divorcing people revert back to a child dependence state. Sometimes it is an attempt to have their personal needs met, and sometimes it is an attempt to make the other person feel guilty. Don't get caught in the trap of assuming responsibility for the former spouse, other than what the law stipulates. Don't spend all your time wondering if the former spouse is going to make it. They will and can make it if they choose to. If they decide to infect themselves with an eternal case of the "woe me's," they will only prohibit their own growth. Don't let them prohibit yours by hooking you into being responsible for them.

4. *Don't let your children intimidate you.* The secret desire of many children is that their parents will get back together again. And that is a natural and acceptable feeling. Children often don't understand the private lives and private wars that adults have. They only know that they want their parents together again.

A child who continually talks about this can inflict a foreboding burden of guilt on a parent. The end result can be a frustrating attempt to fan to life the fires of a long-dead marriage in order to please the child. Remember, you are an adult and children do not always understand adult decisions.

Children have their own ways of getting at a parent. The desired outcome of their intentions might be very honorable, but at a deep level they are probably more concerned that their needs are met than yours.

There are hundreds of games that a child can play to intimidate a parent. A child often begins with statements like: "All my friends have a mother and father who live with them." "Why did you make Daddy (or Mommy) move away?" "Is it my fault that Daddy (or Mommy) doesn't live here anymore?"

These heartrending comments from a child can cause many a parent to race back to a former mate for another try or to fervently pursue a new replacement for the departed parent.

Love and try to understand your children, but don't let them intimidate you.

5. *Don't get trapped in your "child state."* First Corinthians, chapter 13, in the Bible is known as the "love chapter." Verse 11 simply states, "When I was a child, I used to speak as a child, think as a child, reason as a child; when I became a man, I did away with childish things."

It is easy to get trapped into childish behavior with a former spouse. Childish behavior with a "former" may involve temper tantrums, getting even, telling lies, jealousy, fighting, etc. These things can happen when we forget who we are. A child can go from liking a friend to "hating" a friend in the short space of an hour's play. Many adults apparently have the same capacity.

"I love you, I hate you, I'll get you," seems to adequately describe many post-divorce relationships. Vast amounts of mental and physical energies are spent in childish hate campaigns. Arriving five minutes late for visitation or debating about who gets the big-screen television, computer, or super-sound home entertainment equipment can cause once-loving men and women to become violent, warring ones.

Divorce seems a ready catapult that launches people back into their childish behavior patterns. Considerateness, kindness, and honesty are relegated to another place in time. How tragic and demeaning to one's personhood!

Growth in divorce is treating a former spouse as an adult. It is not seeking reprisal and vindication even if you feel deserving of it. Negative and childish treatment of a former mate is immature and a constant drain on your emotional level. Warring people are in a constant state of battle tension. Little positive growth is attained until the fight is declared over.

Becoming an adult means that childish speaking, thinking, and reasoning are abandoned.

In the heat of conflict, argument, and despair we often forget who we are. Divorce is often described as a war with all the tactics and strategy of war put to use. If that is the case, I would plead that the warriors in divorce come to a quick and lasting truce. Nothing is gained by broken and hostile relationships.

If a divorce has to happen, let it become history as quickly as possible and let the relationships of former mates take on a mature form of behavior and existence. Everyone benefits when people are treated with respect and dignity. In your dealings with your former spouse, tell him or her that your part of the war is over. If they continue to fight, let it be their problem and don't continue to supply them with ammunition.

If there's no enemy within,
there's no enemy outside
that can do us any harm!
(African proverb)

Personal Growth and Discussion Questions

1. Which one of the eight basic causes of divorce describes your divorce?

2. Describe your current feelings towards your former spouse.

3. How would you like to feel about your former spouse?

4. Of the 11 issues that involve dealing with your former spouse, which is toughest for you and which is the easiest?

5. Which one of the growth guidelines in getting the former spouse in focus is the most difficult for you? The easiest?

6. Are you currently treating your former spouse as a child or as an adult?

7. My personal goal for this next week is

FOUR

Assuming Responsibility for Myself

"Will somebody out there please make me happy?"

Who is responsible for you and your happiness? Is it your former spouse? Your children? Your boss? Your family? Your friends? God?

Many people would like to give someone else the responsibility for making them happy. It is easy to blame your unhappiness on other people. But reality says that you are responsible for yourself and that it's no one else's job to make you happy.

People often marry other people with the assumption that the person they are marrying will make them happy. What an awesome responsibility is placed upon that person's shoulders! What if they fail? Who gets the blame? Where can other happiness be found? A marriage built upon that premise often leads to a divorce and, unless the lesson is learned, the hunt is on for another person to provide happiness.

Many divorced persons feel that the answer to all their problems will be found in finding the right person. I call this the "abdication of responsibility syndrome." It often leads to a quick second, third, fourth, etc., marriage.

Divorce can be a teacher if you will let it. It will teach you how, as an adult, you can assume responsibility for yourself, your thoughts, and your actions. Persons who grow through divorce experience this. They can go from a marriage that was based on dependency into a divorce that teaches personal responsibility.

A child learns very young that he is spared punishment and responsibility if he can blame his actions or deeds on someone else. We begin to build a pattern in youth that affects our later years. It is easy to come to the place where we always blame someone else for our situation, misdeeds, problems, struggles, lack of growth, or misfortunes. I listen to many people say, "If only I would have…we would not be divorced today." Assuming responsibility for yourself may be a new discovery for you. It begins in the following areas.

1. *I assume responsibility for my part of the failure of my marriage.* One of the insidious traps that divorced persons get caught in is playing the blame game. One or more can play the game, but no one ever wins. Every action in a marriage draws a reaction. Actions and reactions build for years, one person explodes and leaves, and the blame game starts. No one can relive the years of a marriage and change what is history. But accepting responsibility for your part of the failure can certainly change your future. People don't divorce situations; they divorce people who create situations and fail to take responsibility for those situations.

In a divorce, assuming responsibility for yourself does not start with your future—it starts with your past and putting that in perspective. It means expressing your responsibility for the failures in your marriage to your former spouse. If both parties do this, the blame game will come to an end and post-marital relationships will not be warring ones.

2. *I assume responsibility for my present situation.* I frequently hear people blame their present situation, whether it

is housing, lack of money, job, etc., on their past. It is easy to say everything is bad because of what I have just gone through. This kind of situation is known as the "woe me's." Many people get caught in the routine of wishing things were different. They are hooked on extracting pity from others that will reinforce for them the fact that they are merely the victim of circumstances and powerless to handle or change their present situation.

If you do not assume responsibility for your present situation, who will? Part of being an adult is accepting responsibility. If you are a single parent with children at home, a house to maintain, money to earn, a job to pursue, you will not get the job done by endless television-watching, barhopping, chain-smoking, and retreating from life because it has given you a raw deal. Being responsible says you need to assess your present situation and the needs you have. Make a list with the heading at the top reading "I Am Responsible For." Be honest and don't pass the buck. Then draw a line down the center of the page. At the head of the second column write "I Will Fulfill This Responsibility By:" Spend some time on this. Share it with a friend for further input. In effect you are accepting and articulating your responsibilities for right now and setting goals to achieve their fulfillment. Things that are frightening in our mind usually become obtainable realities when placed on paper.

3. *I assume responsibility for my future.* There are many people who live their entire lives with contingency goals. These are not real goals but negative goals that are based upon circumstances and other people. They change constantly as people come and go in our lives. Examples are:

- I won't go to work because I might remarry.
- I won't go back to school because I might fail.

- I won't date because I might get hurt again.
- I won't move because I might not get as good a situation as I have.
- I'll do this until something better comes along.
- I won't set goals because they might interfere with someone I'll meet.

I could add numerous other statements I hear people make every day. Instead of securing their own future with constructive plans and growth-producing goals, they make no moves for fear they will make the wrong ones.

Many people are divorcing today after 20 and 30 years of marriage. When I ask these people what goals they have set for themselves, they often respond by saying it's too late or that their goal is just to survive each day. Someone has said, "Shoot at nothing and that is what you will hit."

No one else is responsible for your future but you. You have to live in it. Accept responsibility for it. Make the best plans for you. Whether you remain single or remarry should not affect your present planning. You do not have to be married to be headed somewhere in life.

4. *I assume responsibility for myself.* During college, we often discussed whether environment or heredity played the biggest part in our personality development. The arguments were good but no one ever seemed to prove one or the other. A fitting conclusion would be that both play a great deal in who we are today. If we are successful today, we can attribute it to our successful influences. Determining causes does not change present realities. Each of us is responsible for ourselves. We cannot renege that responsibility. Three basic areas in self-responsibility are thoughts, feelings, and actions.

Thoughts

What does a divorced person think about?

Why has this happened to me?
What went wrong?
What will I do now?
Can I make it on my own?
How long will I hurt?
Can I ever be happy again?

These and countless hundreds of other thoughts race through your mind every day. Many of these thoughts are negative, self-defeating, and guilt-producing. When negative thoughts build up in the mind, they lead to negative feelings and actions. A divorced person who spends too much time in the negative world runs the risk of becoming lonely, bitter, and depressed. If you spend too much time thinking about all the things that led to your divorce and all the present dangers it has created, your mind will not be free to be constructive and clear in dealing with the realities of today.

Closing the door on the past means closing out the dead thoughts and replacing them with positive thoughts of the present and future. You can control what you think about. For many divorced persons, the lonely hours just prior to or after bedtime trigger thoughts of yesterday or worries about tomorrow.

You can control what you think about! Don't waste mental energy on things you cannot change and have no control over. You are responsible for your thoughts.

Feelings

"How are you feeling?" Fine. Terrible. Tired. Happy. Sad. Depressed. Lonely. Hot. Cold.

Feelings are! I do not choose whether or not to have feelings. They come out of nowhere, sometimes when I am least expecting them. In themselves, feelings are neither good nor bad. I am responsible for what I do with my feelings, but I am not responsible for having them. Everyone has feelings.

But not everyone is in touch with the feelings they have. Being in touch with my feelings means I can identify my feelings and deal with them in a conscious and constructive manner.

Divorced persons have feelings. They have feelings whether they have been wronged or are in the wrong. They have a right to express their feelings.

One of the finest ways to communicate with another person in an area that may raise a conflict is to preface what you are saying with, "My feeling about that is…" Most people come from the judgment side and issue pronouncements rather than simply sharing their feelings.

Here are three things to remember in getting your feelings expressed:

1. Get in touch with the feelings inside you.
2. Develop the freedom to express those feelings.
3. Learn to live comfortably with your feelings.

Feelings need to be identified and expressed. Repressed feelings cause depression, guilt, and hostility toward others. Learn to share your feelings.

Actions

"Stop it! Don't act like that!" "I can't help it. You made me do it!"

How many times as a child did someone reprimand you for your actions, and you tried to place the blame for your actions on someone else? We expect children to react like that, but somehow when we grow up we expect adult behavior. And adult behavior means we assume responsibility for our actions and stop blaming them on other people.

An important key to growth in divorce is assuming responsibility for your actions. Blaming your present actions on another person's treatment of you does not release you from responsibility. Taking charge of yourself means you act on situations rather than react to situations. Check on yourself for a few days and see how many times you are caught reacting rather than acting. Reacting puts the results in someone else's ballpark. Acting keeps them in your ballpark and leaves you in control of the situation. Former mates often spend a great deal of time reacting to each other. Feelings and emotions become so overloaded that there is great, explosive reaction and very little chance for positive action. Reactions trigger defense mechanisms that cause a person to either fight or retreat. Acting on a situation means I hear what is being said, I think about what is being said, and I respond to what is being said. I present a clear statement of my feelings that will lead to my positive actions.

Assuming responsibility for yourself is not an easy process. Like everything else, it takes time. There is no other honest way to face the reality of your divorce. You have to build a new identity and, in order to do that, you have to take charge of yourself. After many years of dependent living, that may be extremely difficult. Divorce will either force you to assume responsibility by saying, "I can," or send you looking for someone else to do it for you.

The following verse describes one person's feelings about rebuilding her life.

My Halfway House

Is in between where I've been and where I'm going.
It's almost a home—especially when someone special comes to
visit halfway between conditions in life
and needs a friend, to listen—A refuge, where
sharing is safe. I feel safe here, although, at times,
I do feel lonely. I've learned many things about
myself—living alone. I'm the same, yet I'm different.
No one can ever replace or be substituted for that
part of me that is gone. My void is being filled in
a new way. I'm becoming—more totally me
halfway between where I've been,
and where I'm going.

—Jan Kruger

Are you just rebounding or are you rebuilding?

Personal Growth and Discussion Questions

1. What are some of the areas in your marriage where you feel you failed?

2. What are some of the struggles you are having in assuming responsibility for your present situation?

3. Are your goals set by you or are they "contingency goals" that are dependent upon other people and situations?

4. In what area do you have the greatest struggle: thoughts, feelings, or actions? Explain.

5. My personal goal for this next week is

FIVE

Assuming Responsibility for My Children

"Divorce is often a war between fathers and mothers. Tragically, children can become the orphans of that war."

Single parenthood usually starts at the moment the children are told that Mommy and Daddy no longer love each other and don't want to continue living in the same house. The announcement to the children of the impending divorce can cause them to give either a sigh of relief or a sob of terror. Inwardly or outwardly, children think about or ask about what will happen to them. Where will they live? With whom will they live? How will things change? Will they ever see the departing parent again? As someone has said, "If divorce can be likened to war, then children are its orphans."

Assuming the responsibility of being a single parent is awesome, frightening, challenging, and rewarding. Few parents embarking upon the experience feel they can do well. But most learn to do it and do a very good job at it. The common fear is that if child-raising was hard with two parents in the home, it will be impossible with only one parent. It takes a great deal of adjusting, but it is not impossible. Assuming and continuing the responsibility of being a single parent is equally important whether you are a weekday mother or father or a weekend mother or father.

Single-Parent Struggles

"My Circuits Are on Overload."

If marriages are strained and overtaxed with the problem of too little money, divorce is equally overloaded with too little money and too many problems. Single parents complain about too many decisions that have to be made without the consultation of another partner, too many jobs to be done by one person that were once divided by two, too many tensions and frustrations that seemingly have only intermediate solutions, and too little time apart from child-rearing to claim as their own. For the parent with custody rights, it's too much children too much of the time. For the parent without custody rights, it's too little children too much of the time. One suffers overload and one suffers loneliness. And the hurt is equal on the emotional level.

Few divorcing partners find the balancing point on the "too much or too little" where the children are concerned. Too often the children become excess baggage to be packed and shuffled from station to station.

"Where Are You When I Need You?"

In many divorce situations, the weekend or visiting parent may become a parent by proxy or consultation only. He or she may only be called upon at a time of crisis, discipline, or decision. Often these needs concern the health of a child, medical or dental decisions, parent/teacher academic needs, or personal behavioral problems of the child. Being a parent by proxy is not easy. Decisions have to be made based only on the facts given, which may or may not be accurate. An absentee parent often has to assume the role of judge.

The custody parent has the problem of contacting and invading the realm of the departed parent with a constant stream of problems. When there are no problems, there is no contact. Resentment can build on both sides. "You are not there when I need you" versus "You only need me when you have a problem." The string of financing is often held by the noncustody parent and used as a weapon to achieve what he or she might want.

"I Don't Get Any Respect."

Divorcing parents can beat each other down verbally to the point where the children lose respect for them and sometimes for themselves. An "out-of-house parent" is seldom around to defend himself or herself from verbal abuse. The very act of leaving the home may force a child to lose respect for the parent. A child may think, "If they loved me, they would not leave." A constant barrage of "Your mother did this" or "Your father did that" is not very affirming in the growth of a child. With the loss of respect comes the problem of getting the children to mind. When respect goes, disobedience is soon to follow. Child discipline can quickly become a problem, and more often than not, the children are left to roam and do as they please.

"Help, I'm a Prisoner."

Single parents can easily become a prisoner of their children. They may overcompensate in every area for the departed parent. They allow their children to restrict their mobility in their social and dating life. If they go out at all, they feel guilty at leaving the children alone or with a sitter. A single parent can allow this to be a serious barrier to personal growth and development.

A parent who confines himself or herself to work and children alone will become a prisoner in his or her own home. Your own emotional health and well-being are important.

Focusing on Your Child's Feelings

Until recent years, children of divorcing parents were kept largely in the background of the divorce issue. Many parents focused on their own needs and feelings while ignoring the reality that their children were going through similar struggles. Fortunately, that has changed and now there are workshops for children of all ages as well as solid educational material. Even with good help, this does not absolve the parent from talking, sharing, and working through the feelings their child has to the divorce and how it will impact his or her life.

There are eight prominent feelings in most children's lives as they go through the divorce experience. These feelings are neither good nor bad. They are just feelings and need to be dealt with and talked through.

1. The foremost feeling with most children is fear. It can involve the unknown as well as the known. Children need to name their fears and have some assurance that their worst nightmare will not come true.

2. Rejection is a close second to fear. Rejection sends the message that one is not loved and may never be loved by anyone again. The Bible tells us that "perfect love casts out fear." I believe that love also gets rid of rejection. You can never tell your children the words "I love you" too many times.

3. Anger swirls through the fear and rejection for many children. I feel that children in their teens probably have more anger to deal with than younger children. I have listened firsthand to a few thousand teens express their anger to me. Anger

is an honest emotion, and hiding it won't help a child's recovery. It needs to be expressed and honored.

4. Abandonment is what many children feel when a parent moves out of the home. Parents need to assure the child that even though Mommy and Daddy live in different places, they will always be there for the child.

5. Powerlessness is a child's feeling that he or she cannot stop the impending divorce or whatever chaos and uncertainty follow it. A child needs to be assured that he will be listened to and considered in any and all decisions that will impact his life and future.

6. Loneliness is a condition that both adults and children will face in their journey through life. For a child living through divorce, it is often acute when he or she has limited contact with one parent or the other who was once a prominent player in the child's life.

7. Guilt is a child's feeling that he or she may have contributed something that caused Mother and Father to get a divorce. Children need to be reassured that the divorce was not caused by them.

8. Loyalty is also up for grabs in a divorce. Children choose the parent they want to side with early in the process. By trying to win the children to their point of view, parents don't often help the situation. Children, in most cases, want to be loyal to both parents and resent one parent putting down the other in front of them.

I have really only touched on a handful of feelings that children experience. My questions to you as a parent right here are, "Do you really know how your children are feeling? Have you spent adequate time talking through their feelings with them?" They may not always want to talk when you want to talk, but you need to keep the door open. If you observe the following guidelines, you will deal with your children's feelings honestly.

Guidelines for Successful Single Parenting

1. *Don't try to be both parents to your children.* Be what you are—a mother or a father. Many single parents make the deadly mistake of trying to fill both parent roles in the family. A single parent assumes some of the jobs the other parent did, but not the role of that parent. Trying to be a superparent will only bring you frustration and fatigue. Inform your children that you have no intention of filling the role of the departed parent but that you are going to work very hard at being the best at what you are. I meet many single parents who are exhausted at trying to do everything and be everything so that their children will not be deprived at having only one parent in the home. Improve what you are and don't try to be what you are not.

2. *Don't force your children into playing the role of the departed parent.* This can start by telling a nine-year-old boy that he has to be the daddy of the house now or by telling a ten-year-old daughter that she is the mommy now. This places an incredible weight on a child's shoulders. Children are forced into playing roles that they neither understand nor are ready for. The desire of the parent is for them to fill in so that they won't have to face the reality of the situation. A child needs to be a child. Children cannot fill an adult's place, so don't force them to. Let them be who they are. Again, they may have to assume some new jobs but not a new personality and identity.

3. *Be the parent you are.* Don't abdicate your parent position for that of a big brother, big sister, friend, buddy, or pal. Some parents want a role change so that they won't have to assume the responsibility of being a single parent. Children have their friends and buddies. They deeply resent having their parent try to invade their world. Single parents who force their way into their children's world are only looking for a way of escape and not for the best interests of their children.

Children need the security of the parent image even more after one parent has left the home. They cannot afford to lose both parents. After divorce, they need to have a parent more firmly in his or her role than ever.

4. *Be honest with your children.* Tell them the truth about what is going on. The Bible tells us to speak the truth in love. I believe that means we tell the truth in a loving framework, remembering that others are connected with our truth. Many single parents never really talk to their children about what has happened, how they feel about it, and how the children feel about it. They may make promises that the other parent will return, that the other parent really loves them, etc., when reality does not bear this out and the parent becomes a liar to the child. Richard Gardner in his book *The Boys and Girls Book About Divorce* is a strong advocate of telling children the truth. He says, "Half-truths produce confusion and distrust, whereas truth, albeit painful, engenders trust and gives the child the security of knowing exactly where he stands. He is then in a better position to handle situations effectively."

5. *Don't put your former spouse down in front of your children.* In most divorces, the parents enter into the never-ending game of trying to convince the children how bad the other parent is and how this divorce is all the other parent's fault. Each parent desperately wants the child to take their side in the conflict. It's a game that nobody wins and that eventually causes the child to lose all respect for either parent. Most children don't really care who did what to whom. What they care about is what is going to happen to them. Let your children decide things for themselves. If you have to talk about your former spouse in front of your children, make it positive, not negative.

6. *Don't make your children undercover agents who report on the other parent's current activities.* Children resent having to

spy on what a parent is doing. Often the reporting back is done by subtle questioning and gentle prying. A good conversation upon the return of a child from being with the other parent would be: "Hi! Did you have a nice time?"

"Yes, we did."

"Good. I'm glad."

A child has the right to privately enjoy a parent. What that person is saying, doing, buying, thinking, etc., is their business. Don't force your children into playing "I Spy."

7. *The children of divorce need both a mother and a father.* Don't deny them this right because of your anger, hostility, guilt, or vengeance.

Some single parents feel that a departing parent has no right to continue the relationship with the children. About the only way a court of law would agree with that would be if the parent might cause emotional or bodily harm to the child. Courts recognize the rights of both parents. One superior court judge in California gives divorcing parents a brochure entitled "Parents Are Forever." Children need the right of access to both parents. Infrequently a parent will give up that right and not want to see the child. In most cases, though, parents feel very strongly about seeing their children. Let your children pursue that relationship as they desire. They will only have one natural mother and father. Don't let the acts or deeds or your feelings about the departed parent deny your child the right to a continuing relationship with that parent.

8. *Don't become an "entertainment parent."* California abounds with entertainment centers. On any weekend of the year, you will find crowds of single parents fulfilling their visitation rights with their children. Tragically, the single parent outside of the home often becomes the entertainer. Not knowing what else to do with the children, taking, buying, and doing seem to provide a way out of the guilt and absence

from the home. As the supply of things to do and places to go becomes exhausted, weekend visits may become less frequent.

Children need to see the departed parent in a real-life setting. Take them to work with you and let them see what you do all day. Make sure they have your work phone number in their wallet or purse. Have them stay overnight at your home or apartment. Let them keep some of their belongings at your residence. If space allows, give them their own room. Let them cook, help with the chores, and be a part of your world. Don't try to buy them. It will make them uncomfortable. It will also put you in the wrong role and be a hard act for the "at home" parent to follow.

9. *Share your dating life and social interests with your children.* After a parent departs the home, any adult that is introduced to the children by either parent is looked upon as a potential new mother or father. If the children are small, they might ask outright, "Are you my new mommy or daddy?" At times, this proves to be embarrassing to both parties. Older children may respond with an aloofness or outright hostility at a potential new parent. Children never ask a parent the question, "How will this affect you?" They want to know how this person might affect them. They want to know how it will affect their relationship with the other parent as well. On the other hand, hiding your date and never informing the children about what is going on will be a greater threat than keeping them informed about your feelings and talking to them openly about the developing relationship.

10. *Help your children keep the good memories of your past marriage alive.* Good memories are worth keeping. They help us become what we are. I recently heard of a single parent who burned all the family pictures that had the other mate in them. You have no right to rob your children of their happy memories. Keep the things that are important to them as well as to

you. If they want to recall good things from the past and talk about them, let them. They have their memories too.

11. *Work out a management and existence structure for your children with your former spouse.* It is a tragedy of our times that the courts become the arbitrators of continuing relationships with children after divorce. Two adults should be able to sit down together and work out things that will encourage the best growth and development of the children. This may not happen in the emotional heat of the pre- and post-divorce setting. But when feelings cool and perspectives are regained, separated parents should be able to face the reality that child-raising goes on and should go on as smoothly as possible for the welfare of the children. Divorce may claim you and your former spouse as its victims. Don't let it claim your children as well. An outside or third-party source such as a divorce counselor can give valuable assistance in helping you set up a management structure for your children.

12. *If possible, try not to disrupt the many areas in your children's lives that offer them safety and security.* The same house, school, friends, church, and clubs will help maintain a balance that can offset to a degree the loss of a parent. Sometimes this is not possible. If a move is forthcoming, talk it over with the children and let them have a part in the decision-making. Present it as an adventure rather than a threat.

13. *If your child does not resume normal development and growth in his or her life within a few months of the divorce, he or she may need the special care and help of a professional family counselor.* During a divorce, a child can become a problem at school, grades can go down, interest in hobbies can vanish, a general attitude of restlessness and disobedience can set in. Some of this is normal. Children go through the stages of shock, adjustment, and growth too. If negative patterns

continue after a number of months, seek help. A few words by a trained professional can often turn the corner of post-divorce adjustment for children.

Being a single parent is a skill to be learned. It is both lonely and rewarding. Many children grow up in one-parent homes and have all the skills and attributes of children who grow up in two-parent homes. Being a single parent does not assure your children of failure or success. A child can grow through divorce too.

The following Bill of Rights for children of divorce was put together by a children's advocate, Virginia Allmaras—a single parent—and some of her friends. We suggest that you copy it and give it to each of your children as your commitment to helping them grow in a healthy way through your divorce.

Bill of Rights

1. The Right to know that I am loved unconditionally.
2. The Right to know that I didn't cause my parents' divorce.
3. The Right to know what caused the divorce.
4. The Right to the security of knowing where I will live and who I will live with.
5. The Right to be aware of how stress affects my life and how I can adapt to it in a healthy way.
6. The Right to be a kid and not to be afraid of being myself.
7. The Right to have the guarantee that my physical and emotional needs will be met.

8. The Right not to be a victim of the past marriage and not to be used as a pawn between my parents.

9. The Right to have my own space for privacy to ensure respect of my person.

10. The Right to have a normal household routine and discipline to warrant a sense of security.

11. The Right to possess positive images of my parents so that I can love each parent equally.

12. The Right to have access and time with each parent equally.

Personal Growth and Discussion Questions

1. How do your children relate to the absentee parent?

2. What is the biggest problem you face in being a single parent?

3. Are you listening to and talking out your children's feelings about your divorce? Share with the group how you feel that is going.

4. How did you tell your children about your divorce? What was their reaction?

5. How do you envision using the Bill of Rights found at the end of this chapter with your children?

6. What kind of picture of your former spouse do you present to your children?

7. My personal goal for this next week is

SIX

Assuming Responsibility for My Future

> *"Plan ahead...you have to live there!"*

I ask many people who are experiencing divorce how they feel about their future. They often reply by saying, "What future?" The response is a natural one. The clouds of emotion, doubt, tension, and the unknown tend to obliterate the thoughts of a clear and promising tomorrow. Planning ahead will seem very unrealistic when your mind is filled with the thoughts of yesterday and the current problems of today. Your future can be a threat or a promise, depending upon your attitude and plans.

Yes, You Have a Future

Unless you die instantly while reading these lines, you will have a future. No one is certain of how long or how short it will be. Growth in divorce is assuming responsibility for your future, whether it is a long one or a short one. A divorced person sometimes has a greater will to die than to live. Death might seem honorable while life seems threatening. But positive planning for your future will give you the excitement of living in today. You have a future and it is entirely up to you to make plans to live in it. It is your responsibility—no one can do it for you. A wise person once said that there are three things that make for happiness in living: something to do, someone to love, and something to look forward to. What are you looking forward to right now?

Stop reading for a few minutes and list five things you are looking forward to in your immediate future.

1.

2.

3.

4.

5.

If you had a hard time making this list, it might be because you are living in the past and have no plans for your future.

There are three kinds of people when it comes to future planning: those who watch things happen, those who make things happen, and those who don't know what's happening. Which one describes you? A person who assumes responsibility for their future is a person who makes things happen by constructive and intelligent planning.

You Can Fly, but That Cocoon Has to Go!

I am confident that there were many skeptics in the crowd that day as the Wright brothers announced they were going to fly. Those who had tried in the past had failed. But the Wright brothers had made their plans, and following them proved to everyone that flying could be a reality for man. But in order to become airborne, the Wright brothers had to leave the safety of the ground behind. Flying is only risky when you take your feet off the ground. Assuming responsibility for your future is only risky when you make plans and follow those plans. And perhaps the biggest risk is that the plans might fail.

Edison did not invent the light bulb on the first try. His attempts were fraught with continued failure for months. But success became a reality for him because he did not give up. The secret of success in any area of life is leaving the security of the known and venturing into the unknown. Divorce launches people from a known world into an unknown world. Sometimes divorce will trick you into believing you left your sound mind and good thinking and planning processes in that other world. But you didn't. You still have them and they still work.

I frequently hear the complaints, "I just can't think straight anymore!" "I'm confused; I just can't make decisions." It is difficult to make sound decisions and plans when you are emotionally low. Consult with trusted and wise friends or counselors when you need help in planning.

Divorce can become a cocoon that you can use to hide in from the challenge of the future. You can pull it around you and let it become your excuse for not facing reality. You can only fly if you shed that cocoon.

Setting Realistic Goals for Yourself

To list all of the possible goals that a person could set would fill hundreds of pages. I want to isolate several areas that always seem of paramount importance in a divorce situation. The urgent "big three" that many people struggle with are money, job, and career or vocation. These often emerge as survival goals. Divorce is always expensive, and people readily agree that there is not enough money to go around. Jobs may change as a result of the divorce or the need for more money. A non-working spouse may be faced with finding a job in a world where he or she has no marketable skills. A career or vocation may change or a new one may have to be established. All three of these areas need to be faced realistically. Constructive plans must be made if consistent growth is to be assured.

1. *Evaluate your present situation.*

Future planning always begins by looking at your present situation. In the money area it means taking an honest look at income and expenses and the establishing of a workable budget. The hope that someone else will take care of you does not lead to independent growth. Child support and spousal support have ways of disappearing or being very inadequate. Marrying a rich prince or princess happens only in fairy tales. Living on welfare and food stamps is dependent living and should be used only when necessary. It is demeaning and will cause a loss of self-worth.

A different lifestyle will dictate a reevaluation of monetary needs. It may mean acquiring some of the basics in life all over again. Many people in divorce are defeated by losing some of the things they have taken years to build. Things can evaporate and change overnight. Financial security can turn into financial insecurity. It is easy to give up hope. It is hard to begin again.

In the job area, you may be faced with having to find one. If you have not worked for years, you may wonder if you have anything to give in exchange for a paycheck. During a divorce, a person's self-confidence level is usually very low. Ability to do even a menial job is questioned. It may seem easier to do nothing than to do something.

Explore the possibility of a job that is unpressured and will help you build the confidence you need for something better down the road. The pay may not be that great and there may be little prestige, but you have to start somewhere. Look upon a first job as a step into your future, not a dead end.

Consult various job-placement agencies, and take job interest and inventory skills tests to see what jobs you might have natural interest and abilities for. Not knowing what you want to do or be is not an excuse for doing nothing. Every person has talents and abilities. Many are untapped and undiscovered. Become a student of job openings and job opportunities. The career area is where good job planning and growth will eventually lead. Having a job means you put in time and receive remuneration for that time. Having a career means having identity, prestige, and respect. You are not just doing something…you are something!

Careers don't just happen—they are planned. They are not contingent upon circumstances, fate, or luck.

Marriage may be the only career or vocation some people have ever had. It may be the only thing they feel they can do. When the marriage dissolved, their career ended.

But marriage is not a career or vocation. It is not the only way to live life. A career is something you discover yourself. You can always have it if you choose to. You can grow in it, expand upon it, and receive unlimited satisfaction in doing it.

Remember the question you were asked as a child: "What do you want to be when you grow up?" Most children answer with great dreams and lofty ideals. Some people never get to do what they want because they never make plans and follow them. Other individuals just never grow up.

As you evaluate your present state, look carefully at your money situation, job situation, and career destination. Start making plans to get where you want to be. Follow the plans that you make. Be willing to make changes as you go.

2. *Explore new and potential situations.*

What makes a person an explorer? The thrill of discovering what's around the next bend in the river or on the other side of the mountain.

Children are great explorers. At a young age, their curiosity has not been tempered by the threat of danger. They are thrilled by new discoveries. They want to try all the new things and discover new joys. Then maturity and caution take over and exploration often becomes a threat.

Setting goals for your future will make you an explorer and an adventurer. It will put the thrill of the unknown back into your daily existence.

New situations need not be approached as threatening. Decide that you are exploring and can take what you want and leave what you want. You are considering alternatives.

When you explore a new situation, make a list of the potential positives and negatives of the situation and how each might affect you.

A divorce is like learning to walk all over again. At first you crawl, then you walk (with a little help and support from others), and then you run. Assuming responsibility for your future is setting you free to explore new things, new ideas, new situations.

3. *Establish short-term and long-term goals.*

Most of us want things to happen now. We don't want to wait until tomorrow, next week, or next year. We fail to set goals for the future because we don't want to wait for the future to arrive. Constructive goal-setting is the ability to reach future goals by experiencing the excitement and incentive of short-term goals.

Let's suppose you wanted to become a schoolteacher but you only finished one year of college prior to your marriage. Your long-term goal would be becoming a teacher. Your short-term goals would involve the steps to attaining that. The first might be enrolling and going back to school. The second short-term goal might be getting good grades the first semester to prove you could do it. A third short-term goal might be to mentally tune your mind to the new world of academia.

Goals can be set on a day-to-day basis, week to week, month to month, or year to year. They need to be attainable so that you can experience the success and positive reinforcement that they bring. Reaching goals says, "I'm going somewhere. I have a plan and a purpose." Many divorced people bob along through life like corks on the water. They have no plan or purpose and their goals, if any, are largely contingent upon whoever might walk into their life.

Having short-term and long-term goals will help you get up in the morning excited and go to bed at night satisfied. Your purpose in life will not be tied to another person but to the goals and objectives you have set up for yourself.

4. *Don't be afraid of commitments.*

"A marriage ceremony is where promises are made, married life is where they are lived out, and a divorce is where they are broken." This is how one person described her life.

Many people look back on an unhappy marriage where commitments were not kept and decide that they will never make commitments again. They become "commitment shy" in many areas of their life because they have been hurt.

It is easy to build a shrine around your hurt and spend the rest of your days worshiping at it. Broken commitments in your past must not keep you from making new commitments in your future. Past failures do not mean future failures unless we failed to learn from the past. The fear of failing keeps many people from making commitments in the areas of job, career, new responsibilities, and new relationships. No one wants to be hurt and no one wants to fail. But the reality of life is that we will be hurt at times and we will fail at times. Growth teaches you how to learn by your experiences.

Making any commitment is not easy. It is a decision of the mind and the will. It is lived out by the actions of the person making it. Being a responsible adult means living up to your commitments. Taking responsibility for your future means making a commitment to plan for it.

Ten Commandments for Formerly Marrieds

- Thou shalt not live in thy past.
- Thou shalt be responsible for thy present and not blame thy past for it.
- Thou shalt not feel sorry for thyself indefinitely.
- Thou shalt assume thy end of the blame for thy marriage dissolvement.
- Thou shalt not try to reconcile thy past and reconstruct thy future by a quick, new marriage.
- Thou shalt not make thy children the victims of thy past marriage.
- Thou shalt not spend all thy time trying to convince thy children how terrible and evil their departed parent is.

- Thou shalt learn all thou can about being a one-parent family and get on with it.
- Thou shalt ask others for help when thou needest it.
- Thou shalt ask God for the wisdom to bury yesterday, create today, and plan for tomorrow.

5. *Trust God with your future.*

In the Ten Commandments for Formerly Marrieds, the tenth commandment is "Thou shalt ask God for the wisdom to bury yesterday, create today, and plan for tomorrow."

Trusting God with your future is inviting God to direct your conscious thoughts and plans as you set goals and objectives for your future. It is asking God for His wisdom in your planning and projecting. It is living with the confidence that God is in charge of your life today and He will be in charge of tomorrow too. Trusting God with your future does not mean you fail to plan for it. Some people do nothing and hope God will do everything. God has given you a mind to use. He does not expect us to be inane robots who never think and who act only upon command. The Scriptures tell us in 2 Timothy 1:7 (KJV) that "God hath not given us the spirit of fear; but of power, and of love, and of a sound mind." God expects us to use our sound mind in planning and setting goals for our future.

Trusting God with your future does not mean that it will be free of troubles and problems. It does mean that you have someone to take the troubles and problems to when they happen. It does not always mean that you will like what is happening, but it does mean you can trust God with what is happening.

Your future can be your friend or your enemy. You can move creatively and constructively toward it by formulating goals and objectives. It's your future. Plan ahead…you have to live there!

Always remember, there is no growth without some pain!

Personal Growth and Discussion Questions

1. Discuss what goals you would like to set for yourself in the following areas:

   Money

   Job

   Career

2. Develop a series of five to seven goals for yourself for the next one to six months. After you have written your list here, rewrite it and place it on your refrigerator door.

   1.

   2.

   3.

   4.

   5.

   6.

   7.

3. If you knew that you could not fail, what would you attempt to do?

4. What are the biggest problems you have in setting and reaching your goals?

5. Discuss honestly how you feel right now about your future.

6. My personal goal for this next week is

SEVEN

Finding a Family

---

*"Having a family means
you belong to someone."*

Contemporary society has two distinctive traits. It is couple-oriented and family-inclined. As I am writing this, it is the month of June and, as a minister, I will perform a number of weddings during this month. All of these weddings will involve a man and a woman joining together in the sharing of wedding vows and commitments. In the eyes of the state, God, family, and friends, they will officially become "couples." For many of them, a natural outgrowth of that coupling process will be the bearing of children. Two people are a couple. Two people with a child or children are a family.

If the above is true, would it be logical to say that if one mate or the other leaves the family through divorce, it is not a family anymore? No, I don't think so. But many of us think of family only in a generic sense or a living-together sense.

Having a family means you belong to someone. You have a supportive group of people around you who accept you, care about you, love you, and support you.

Divorce uproots and dismembers families. It can cause the members of that family to feel family-less. It is vitally important that a sense of family and support are maintained through divorce.

I want to share with you in this chapter three kinds of families and how a sense of knowing you belong to a family can help you grow through divorce.

The Family You Were Born Into

The first family that you became aware of was the family that you were born into. It probably consisted of a mother, father, brothers, sisters, along with other relatives. No one consulted you while you were a struggling embryo and asked you what family you wanted to be born into. You had no choice in the matter whatever. And once you arrived into that family, the family itself had no choice on whether or not to keep you or send you back for a different model. You were there and they were there. They had to begin accepting you and you had to begin accepting them. They made you feel loved, wanted, and comfortable long before you could exchange that same feeling for them.

Many of the thoughts and feelings about family that you have today probably came as a result of your experiences in the family you were born into and grew up in. Looking back, you may assess some of those experiences as good and some as bad, some as negative and some as positive. Regardless of your feelings, it was your earthly family and it brought you into this life.

Reflecting back on your earthly family, think about these four questions for a few minutes.

- How does or did that family receive you?
- How did you or do you receive it?
- What did it do for you?
- What did you do for it?

Your earthly family was your introduction to people on this earth. From it you either found support and love or you were denied these. Hopefully, you gave something to your family and it gave something to you.

The Family That You Married Into

With family and friends around you, you stood one day at a new point in your life. You made the decision to marry and establish a new family. In order to do this, you left the old one behind and placed your priorities and attentions in the new one. You did not abandon the old family; you added a new one by choice. It started with two people, and perhaps more quickly than you wanted, it became three. It was your family; you created it by your choice. You dreamed your dreams and set your goals.

You injected into it all that you had learned from your own family. In looking back on this second family in your life, think about these questions for a few minutes.

- What dreams do you or did you have for this family?
- Have those dreams been fulfilled?
- Do you still feel a part of that family?
- Do you feel family-less since your divorce?

The family that you married into may not have fulfilled your expectations. Your divorce may have left you disenchanted with the whole idea of family. It may have embittered you and left you looking for a family that would not change by whim or with a change of mind. You may be questioning the whole concept of a family right now and wondering if you can ever feel the love, warmth, and support of one again.

The family that you were born into can be taken from you through death. You can move away from the old home, family, and friends. Distance can lessen the importance that family plays in your life. Divorce can cause you to lose the family you married into and sometimes, because of feelings and misunderstandings, your natural family may become very remote in your life as well.

The experience of losing family after having it can be traumatic. The struggle to regain a sense of family and identify with one is even more difficult.

God's Family

In our divorce-recovery workshops across the country, we teach people that there is a third family that they can become a part of. This family is the family of God.

If you have had little or no experience with God in your life, it may seem strange to think about the family of God in a sense of personal belonging. You may not see it as taking the place of an earthly family. Let me share with you some distinctives about the family of God that you may never have thought of.

1. God's family is a "forever family." It is permanent and unchanging. It is unlike your earthly family or your marriage family. You can lose them by death, distance, deed, or divorce. Once you decide to become a part of God's family, you are a member for all time and eternity. In 1 Peter 2, verses 9 and 10, there is a promise concerning this:

> But you are a chosen race, a royal priesthood, a holy nation, a people for God's own possession, that you may proclaim the excellencies of Him who has called you out of darkness into His marvelous light; for once you were not a people, but now you are the people of God; you had not received mercy, but now you have received mercy.

2. You can join God's family by receiving and recognizing His Son, Jesus Christ, as the new Director of your life. When you were a child, one of the first words you learned to speak was "da-da." As you grew older it became "Daddy," then perhaps "Dad" or "Father." You slowly came to associate that name with love, correction, caring, instruction, provision, protection. The longer you knew Dad, the more he meant in your life. You received him into your growing life because you understood that he cared for you and loved you.

The very same principle is true when you give your life to Christ. You learn to trust Him and love Him because He daily shows those same things to you. You build a relationship with Him in a day-by-day walk with Him. He means something to you and you mean something to Him.

3. You grow each day you are part of this family. Many people who decide to become part of God's family have many questions.

Growth and knowledge are only achieved as we live each day. When a person decides to follow Christ and be a part of God's family, he needs to learn everything he can about the person he is following and about how that family functions. Some of this comes by study, worship, prayer, and talking to other members of the family. It comes slowly but surely and in much the same way that growth came about as you learned more about your earthly father and what he expected from you.

God is never in a hurry. He has lots of time. He would like to walk beside you and help you in your journey through life.

4. When you join the family of God, you join as a brother or sister and you inherit all the other people who have joined before you as your new brothers and sisters. That's joining a pretty large family! There is no larger family in existence than God's family. What a sense of belonging that can give you. You

may feel alone, empty, friendless, and family-less. But when you join the family of God, you have instant family and a supportive fellowship that will accept you as you are and struggle with you and grow with you. They will be with you in the happy moments as well as the sad ones. They will extend a love to you that will be beyond even that of your own families at times. Joining the family of God is joining the "loving bunch," as someone recently described it.

5. You have responsibilities to all the other members in this family just as they have responsibilities to you. Remember when your father or mother assigned you your first chores? You really thought you were somebody. For years you had mimicked the jobs your parents did in your play world. Finally they assigned you some real jobs and you zealously went about them each day—until they became routine, mundane, and boring. Then you tried to avoid them. But somehow it never quite worked and you still had to do them. You had a job to uphold your end of the family's responsibilities.

Don't mistake this kind of responsibility with what we were speaking about in the other chapters. I said that you were not responsible for other people and their actions. In the family of God, you are responsible to other members in living out with them the Christian lifestyle. You are responsible to:

• Accept them as brothers and sisters.
• Accept them as they are.
• Share your life with them.
• Love them, support them, and help them when possible.
• Affirm them with the love of Christ.

They, in return, are responsible to care for you in the same way. The apostle Paul put it in these words: "Therefore encourage one another, and build up one another, just as you also are doing" (1 Thessalonians 5:11).

6. You can't "unjoin" this family. There are many ways of losing relationships in your earthly family. There are many ways of breaking relationships with the family you married into. Divorce is one of those ways. A lawyer, a piece of paper, and a pronouncement by a judge, and it's all over. How does a person get a divorce from God? Is there such a thing? I don't believe there is. The Scriptures state these words by Jesus: "And the one who comes to Me I will certainly not cast out" (John 6:37).

Once we come to God and give our life to Christ, we receive the promise that God will not cast us away or turn His back on us. This does not mean that we cannot or will not turn our back on Him. We can drift from God by our own choice. We can shrug off our responsibilities to grow and have a relationship with God in name only. That would be comparable to having family privileges without family responsibilities.

Many people who have gone through a divorce have lost the warmth and closeness of family. They lack a supportive community of people around them who genuinely care about them and what happens to them. An indispensable part of our successful program for formerly married persons is helping people care for people. This is accomplished by letting people know that there is a place in our midst where they can find acceptance, caring, and love. They are welcomed into a group of people who have shared in similar experiences and who have discovered for themselves that life does not end at divorce. Through small-group discussion programs, seminars, workshops, personal counseling, and biblical teaching, many people who are left with the feeling that no one cares find in reality that many people here really do care. Help is given in bringing the formerly married back to emotional strength and health. Practical assistance is given in meeting the everyday demands of making life work. A strong spirit of family is in evidence as the members of our varied age groups intermingle in the areas of mental, social, physical, and spiritual growth each week.

The spirit that pervades our ministry to the formerly married is the Spirit of Christ. It is the spirit of acceptance and forgiveness that we will speak about in the next chapter. There are people who care deeply about you and want you to know the love that they know by being a part of the family of God. These words describe how some join our family and God's family:

I Came Searching

Out of my lonely place, I came searching.
Out of my hidden fears, I came searching.
Out of my need for friends, I came searching.
Out of my quest for God, I came searching.
And I found a people who care, and a new love to share.

How can I find a supportive fellowship?

Making a commitment of your life to Christ and joining God's family is the key part of a new beginning for you. Once you have reached this decision, it is important that you become a part of a group of people who have shared your experience and are trying to go in the same direction as you are.

There are many good groups across the country that will fill your days with mental, social, and physical pursuits geared to the divorced person. There are very few that offer fellowship and support in the spiritual area. The agency in our world that can and should offer help in all four areas is the church. Many churches, however, frown upon having divorced persons in their midst, while other churches simply do not see the need for it.

Make an appointment with a minister you might know or one who might be receptive to you and explore the possibility of starting a group to minister to the needs of the formerly married persons in your community. Once the word gets out that you are offering an alternative to the bar scene, you will have people climbing the walls to get in and share in an authentic fellowship that has a purpose.

It's not easy, but the rewards of ministering to the needs of formerly married persons are immensely satisfying. I can speak from personal experience for that is my job.

"For I know the plans I have for you," declares the Lord, "plans to prosper you and not to harm you, plans to give you hope and a future."
Jeremiah 29:11 (NIV)

Personal Growth and Discussion Questions

1. Describe the kind of relationship you have today with the family that you were born into.

2. How did your family feel about your divorce?

3. How did your divorce affect your concepts and feelings about family?

4. If you have a supportive family around you, describe how you feel about it and how it helps you.

5. Have you become a member of God's "forever family"? If you have, describe how that happened to you.

6. My personal growth goal for this week is

EIGHT

Finding and Experiencing Forgiveness

"I'm not perfect. I'm just forgiven!"

In the recovery process of working through a divorce, there is an area that many people are reluctant to deal with. It is the area of finding and experiencing forgiveness. A person can learn to deal with the many aspects of being divorced on a mechanical level, but the area of forgiveness must be dealt with on a spiritual level.

In the religious community, divorce has stood for a long time as the somewhat unforgivable sin. The Bible does not teach this, but the church has somehow convinced a lot of people that it does. Divorce often becomes a worse sin than stealing or murder. A divorced person is looked upon as permanently marred, bruised, tainted, or condemned. Although these viewpoints seem very medieval and un-Christlike, they are experienced by many people who have gone through a divorce.

Our purpose in this chapter is not to change the attitude of the religious community toward the divorced person. That is slowly happening in many areas. Whether or not the religious community or your church forgives you is not that important.

What is important is that you know and experience personal forgiveness.

Forgiveness Gets the Hate Out

I don't know of any other experience in life outside of divorce that can stretch a person's emotions and feelings from love to hate. Divorce can cause you to build walls in your life in place of bridges. You can start out hating a former spouse and end up hating yourself and everyone around you. You can literally drown yourself in a sea of negative feelings toward other people and yourself. This kind of emotional bath can keep you from growing and becoming a new person.

Time diminishes hate but it does not heal it. Experiencing forgiveness gets the hate out of your life permanently. There are several areas in knowing forgiveness that I would like to share with you.

God Forgives Me!

I believe that one of the greatest therapies that God ever gave to man was the therapy of forgiveness. Without it, we would live in a constant state of guilt that could never be removed. Jesus set the stage for this in the Scriptures. In the Gospel of John, chapter 8, Jesus is confronted with some religious leaders of His day who have brought a woman to Him. The charge is that she was caught in the act of adultery. You will not read very far in this chapter before you will decide that the religious leaders were bent upon exacting punishment while Jesus was concerned about enacting forgiveness to the woman. In the last verse of this biblical incident, Jesus speaks to the woman with these words: "Neither do I condemn you; go your way. From now on sin no more."

What I see happening here sets an example of how we can look at other people's mistakes and how God deals with those mistakes. Jesus did not penalize the woman. He forgave her and encouraged her to begin living a new kind of life.

The religious leaders would have made an example of her to others. Jesus understood man's humanity and imperfections far better than those who were supposed to be the priests to men.

The Scriptures contain numerous accounts of how Jesus dealt with human weakness. He expressed disappointment at it many times, but He never condemned it. He was in the forgiveness business. In response to the disciples' request for an example of prayer, Jesus included the words "Forgive us our trespasses as we forgive those who trespass against us." Forgiveness is reciprocal. In 1 John, chapter 1, verse 9, we read, "If we confess our sin, He is faithful and righteous to forgive us our sins and to cleanse us from all unrighteousness." This verse is a promise that lets us know we can be forgiven if we admit our sin.

I believe divorce is a sin. It was not a part of God's perfect plan for man. But man in his weakness and humanity cannot always live up to God's ideal. The standards for man are set by God. When man breaks the standard, he must have a way to experience God's forgiveness and be restored to fellowship with God.

Dr. Dwight Small in an article entitled "Divorce and Remarriage: A Fresh Biblical Perspective" states,

> All divorce is failure to meet God's standard and hence it is sin; all parties alike need God's grace. But to all divorced Christians, guilty as well as innocent, renewing grace is available. The sole condition is true penitence, confession, and the sincere desire to go on to fulfill God's purpose.

Experiencing God's forgiveness begins by confession of our weakness and wrongdoing.

Remember when you were a child and you disobeyed your parents? Perhaps you covered it up for a time and they did not know about it. But you knew and you lived with the threat of being discovered and punished. Added to that was the weight of a guilty conscience. When you finally confessed your wrongdoing, you experienced a great sense of relief and the good feeling that everything was all right again between you and your parents.

The same good feeling prevails when we make things right with God. Here is a simple prayer that may express how you feel. Take a moment and share it with God.

God, I know that divorce is wrong.
I know it was not Your ideal for me.
God, I confess to You my weaknesses and
human failings that contributed knowingly
and unknowingly to my divorce.
God, I ask Your forgiveness for my
divorce. Help me to know and experience
Your love through Your forgiveness. Lead me
to new growth and new beginnings in my life.
Thank You, Lord! Amen.

I Forgive Me!

The second part of experiencing forgiveness is the most difficult for many people. It is easier to confess our humanity before God than it is to admit it to ourselves. We live by the motto: "I'm not perfect, but just don't remind me of it." It is extremely hard to admit our own weaknesses and shortcomings.

The finest court in the land could not examine all the intricacies that combined to cause a marriage to fail. Few counselors are skilled enough to assess who or what caused the marriage to disintegrate. Lacking a pronouncement of some form that would place the blame, many people who go through a divorce take the blame upon themselves. Others might tend to absolve themselves of all blame.

Many people who experience divorce cannot forgive themselves for whatever part they played in the process. They end up playing the game of "If only I'd..." There is no way you can win this game because you can't change anything. What has happened is history.

Forgiving yourself means:
- I accept my humanity as a human being.
- I have the freedom to fail.
- I accept responsibility for my failures.
- I can forgive myself for my failures.
- I accept God's forgiveness.
- I can begin again.

Many people live under the yoke of self-imposed guilt. They are unable to accept the fact that to be human means you will make mistakes. Until they can experience the refreshing climate of self-forgiveness, they will not enjoy their humanity.

I Forgive My Former Spouse

I can hear you saying, "Now that's carrying things too far! After all that he or she has done to me, I will never forgive my former spouse."

When a person is caught in the heat of argument and emotional combat, forgiveness is usually the very last happening to come to mind. Be aware that forgiveness is not an instant happening but a process that you grow into. Few people that I have shared these thoughts with in divorce-recovery seminars have raced out of the class to see if they work. Forgiveness from God comes easiest and is the first step. Self-forgiveness is second and is a little harder. Forgiveness in the former spouse realm is usually a long way down the recovery road and can only happen when the fires of divorce cool long enough to let sound thinking take over.

A person asked me recently what to say to a former spouse in this area. You might start by saying, "I'm sorry. I ask your forgiveness for all my mistakes and whatever part I might have played in contributing to our divorce." Sounds hard, doesn't it? It is. But the personal sense of growth and well-being that comes from doing it makes it worthwhile.

Asking forgiveness of a former spouse is admitting your weaknesses and the contributions you made to the divorce. It is saying that you were a part of the marriage and a part of the divorce. It is also recognizing the worth of another person and that they are forgivable.

Many post-divorce relationships remain hostile and tense for years. Forgiving a former spouse means asking forgiveness for your wrongs and also giving forgiveness to the former spouse for their wrongs. Remember, you are only accountable for yourself. It is not your job to remind others of their wrongs so that they can ask you to forgive them.

My Former Spouse Forgives Me

What if they don't? You have just put yourself on the line and asked for forgiveness. The response may not have been what you hoped for. Forgiveness was refused, treated lightly, laughed at, or just ignored. What do you do now? Nothing! You have fulfilled your part of the responsibility. You cannot elicit or control the responses you want from other people. If they choose to ignore you, then you must let it be their problem. You can be confident that you have done all that you can and the rest is up to them.

Forgiving and Forgetting

I have listened to many people tell me that they can forgive but they will never forget. And I would agree that on their own strength forgetting will be hard, if not impossible. I believe that the forgetting of things must be left up to God. We all know that time is a healer and time causes us to forget. As tensions and hurts are erased through seeking forgiveness, I believe we slowly forget the bad things and remember the good. You can always take personal action in the forgiveness realm. You will have to trust God and time with the forgetting area.

God is in the business of introducing people to new beginnings. His method of doing this is to bring healing and wholeness into lives through struggle and growth.

The Scriptures teach unlimited forgiveness. In Matthew 18:22, Jesus states that we forgive "seventy times seven." That does not mean we forgive 490 times and quit. It means that God's forgiveness and ours should be unlimited.

Divorce can be shattering and devastating, but it is not unforgivable. I believe that God looks upon the millions of lives that have been deeply wounded by divorce and wants to bring into those lives the fresh breezes of His love and forgiveness.

It can happen to you! You won't be perfect, but you will be forgiven!

Prayer for the Divorced

God, Master of Union and Disunion, Teach me how I may now walk Alone and strong. Heal my wounds; Let the scar tissue of Thy bounty Cover these bruises and hurts That I may again be a single person Adjusted to new days. Grant me a heart of wisdom, Cleanse me of hostility, revenge and rancor, Make me know the laughter

which is not giddy, The affection which is not frightened. Keep far from me thoughts of evil and despair. May I realize that the past chapter of my life Is closed and will not open again. The anticipated theme of my life has changed,
The expected story end will not come. Shall I moan at the turn of the plot? Rather, remembering without anger's thrust Recalling without repetitive pain of regret,
Teach me again to write and read That I may convert this unexpected epilogue Into a new preface and a new poem.
Muddled gloom over, Tension days passed,
Let bitterness of thought fade Harshness of memory attenuate Make me move on in love and kindness.

(Source unknown)

"Forgiveness is surrendering my right
to hurt you back if you hurt me."
Dr. Archibald Hart

Personal Growth and Discussion Questions

1. If you have experienced God's forgiveness in your divorce, describe how this came about and what brought you to it.

2. Where are you in the struggle to forgive yourself?

3. If you have asked your former spouse for forgiveness, what happened? If you have not, how do you feel about doing it?

4. Describe an experience from your life where you wanted forgiveness and received or did not receive it.

5. How are you handling the "forgetting" in your divorce?

6. My personal growth goal for this week is

NINE

47 Going on 17

---

*"I resent...having to act, think,
and date like a 17-year-old again."*

A person's social existence is drastically altered by divorce. The divorced person no longer seems to fit the world of the married. Social contacts and social calendars change abruptly when people separate. A divorced person is tossed from the security of always having a special someone there to having no one there. If they intend to continue socializing in the human race, they are forced to go out with members of the same sex or they are forced to go to bars, clubs, and singles' groups and compete for the attention of members of the opposite sex. The singles' world can be a scary world and can send you running back to the security of your home or apartment. Little wonder that so many singles are in hiding.

In a recent conversation, a divorced person shared this comment with me: "I resent being 47 years of age and having to act, think, and date like a 17-year-old again." Most formerly married people that I meet share those sentiments. And yet, if a person is to have a social life, meet new friends, and establish new relationships, he or she will have to date.

Some people coming out of a divorce decide to jump right into the dating game and try to quickly establish a new relationship that leads to a new marriage. They are propelled by their own insecurity and fear of being alone. It is a mistake to jump into any kind of relationship until you have had time to adjust to your divorce and the new demands it has placed upon you.

Building a New Relationship...The Fears

There are six questions that I hear people ask as they consider building a new relationship with the opposite sex.

1. *Can I be sure it will last this time?*

There are no guarantees in building a new relationship. Even if you feel you have stretched, struggled, healed, and grown for a few years after divorce, it is easy to be on the defensive and become relationship shy. Many men and women are so hurt by their divorce that they fend off any new relationship at all, fearing another rejection. Other people set a record for emotional collisions, hoping they will meet someone who will make all their pain disappear and set a rainbow over their life.

Any new relationship is a risk. All a person can do is learn from past experience and walk hopefully into the future while slowly learning to trust again.

2. *Can I ever trust another man or woman again?*

All people are not the same. If you are hurt or lose trust in one person, it does not mean that everyone will treat you the same. All men are not bad. All women are not bad. It is very unfair to develop a distrust of the opposite sex in general just because of a bad experience you have had. Trust grows over a period of time. Lasting relationships don't develop overnight. Some formerly marrieds want instant friendships or marriages without developing trust levels.

3. Will I make the same mistakes again?

Not if you learn by them and give yourself time to grow. It generally takes a person from two to three years to get a perspective on their divorce and learn the needed lessons from it. In sports, good coaching and good practice eliminates bad habits and mistakes. An honest evaluation of the mistakes you might have made in your marriage will help you learn from them. Blaming the other party will not help you learn anything. Facing your mistakes honestly will help you learn. Most people learn by trial and error. Most will admit the trials but too few admit the errors. If you don't correct your mistakes, you will take them into another marriage and make them all over again.

4. Can I be happy if I marry again?

People have been trying to define happiness for years. It means different things to different people. Many people look for that special person to make them happy. They don't want to assume the responsibility for themselves. They want someone else to assume it. Happy people attract happy people. Happiness is more internal than external. If you work on your own happiness level, you will take happiness into a new relationship. Being married does not ensure happiness any more than being single does.

5. What if I don't find someone?

National statistics indicate that 90 percent of all divorced persons remarry. With the averages on your side, the chances are very likely that you will remarry someday. Hopefully you will wait until you can put your life back together and grow from the experience of your divorce. Women frequently ask where all the good, eligible men are. The men ask where all the good, eligible women are. One thing is for sure—they are not all hiding in the same place. There are good people everywhere. You will find them if you take the time to look.

There are some people who will choose not to remarry, and this is a personal choice. Not everyone should be married and not everyone should be single. Every individual should evaluate what is best for them.

6. *Will I feel confident and sure enough to begin dating?*

It is not easy to start a dating life after being married for 10, 20, 30, or 40 years. In many instances, it's not a case of being too old, but too rusty. Remembering what to say, what to do, where to go, and how to act is not easy when you have lived a long time with only one person. Dating after many years of a married existence will be as scary for you as it is for your 14-year-old son or daughter. You build confidence as you go. And unless you decide to remain single the rest of your life, you will have to enter the dating world.

Building a New Relationship…The Cautions

There are always some caution flags to be raised in the world of post-divorce dating. The following questions will help you examine some of the cautions.

1. *Have I learned anything about me through my divorce?* Everyone should write their own short book bearing the title *Lessons My Divorce Has Taught Me*. The opening chapters should deal with the things you have learned about yourself. Part of the growth process in divorce is learning who you are.

If you jump into post-divorce dating without evaluating what you have learned about yourself, your strengths, and your weaknesses, you might be setting yourself up for another fall. For a person in their first post-divorce dating relationship, there is a great risk that if that relationship does not end in marriage, they will suffer the same emotional shock upon a breakup as they did in their divorce. Take some time to evaluate what you have learned about yourself through your divorce.

2. *Has enough time elapsed to let the dust settle?* Previously we mentioned that it takes from two to three years for the dust to settle in most people's lives, depending upon how long you were married. Proving to a former mate that you are still desirable by a quick new marriage won't help that dust to settle. Give yourself all the time you need and then some. The greatest mistake of divorced persons is to remarry too quickly.

3. *Am I building healthy relationships?* A good marriage is one where both parties are interdependent. A healthy relationship is not a leaning one where one person drains the other. Each person has to contribute something in the building of a healthy relationship. In a healthy relationship, there is a balance between giving and receiving. A good rule would be to date people who are at least as far removed from their divorce as you are. They will have had time to get their own life in order.

In many singles' groups there are people who prey upon emotionally weaker people to meet their own ego needs. No matter how shaky you feel on the emotional level, avoid these people like the plague. A healthy relationship can be established when both parties are growing and have come to terms with their own divorce.

4. *How much of my past marriage am I dragging into my new relationship?* You will know you are gaining in your own growth and post-divorce adjustment when you talk less and less about your former marriage, spouse, and divorce. People who are recovering from their divorce usually don't want to keep hearing divorce stories. If you spend your dating hours rehashing your divorce, you are dragging excess baggage along with you. If you don't get it behind you, you may bring it with you into a new marriage. Leave the past in the past and concentrate on new beginnings with new goals and new dreams.

Building a New Relationship...The Trusts

The sign on the wall said, "In God we trust—all others pay cash." It conveyed the level of trust that the restaurant owners had with their clientele. It is easy to trust God. He has a good track record. It is usually harder to trust people because they can let you down.

In the world of relationships, each of us has some kind of relationship with God, with ourselves, and with the people around us. Each day we work at building those relationships.

Divorce shatters these relationships and causes us to doubt their security and validity. Building new relationships begins with the help of God in the following areas.

1. *With my trust in God and with His help, I can begin again.* Rebuilding England from the ruins after the severe bombings in World War II was a major job. Without the undying determination of the British people, England would still be in ruins. Building a life when it appears in ruin is not easy, and it will take the best determination you can find. God is not in the business of applauding your failures. He wants you to put

your trust in Him and be about the business of new beginnings.

2. *With the help of God, I can learn to love and trust in new ways.* Love and trust sometimes evaporate completely during a divorce. Rebuilding them becomes a mammoth undertaking. The fear of loving again and being hurt may cause you to give up trying. Bertrand Russell said, "To fear love is to fear life and those who fear life are already three parts dead." You may feel dead, but you are alive. With the daily help of God you will learn to love and trust in new ways.

3. *I will trust that God is doing a new work in my life and will continue to do it. If and when I remarry, it will be the richest experience of my life.* Remarriage for some people is an option, while for others it is an opportunity.

If God is at work in your life, it will be a great opportunity. At our church, an exciting group of people meet for study and fellowship each week. They all have one thing in common: They have been married before. They all walked through the valley of divorce and struggled up the mountain of recovery on the other side. They know the hurt, the heartache, the loneliness that divorce can bring. But they were not defeated by it. They worked at rebuilding their lives by forming new relationships. Those relationships have led to marriage and a rich new experience for these people. They share their struggles, joys, and pain as they work to make their marriages work. The next chapter will deal with some of the problems they face.

The dating, relating, and mating of divorced persons can be one of the most difficult areas that you may face in growing through your divorce. You may alternately run to it and run from it. You may despair of so many dates and relationships that seem meaningless. You may feel like a piece of merchandise in an open-air market. But don't let what you feel influence what you are. You are on the way to rebuilding

your life. Day by day you are putting new blocks into place.
God is doing a new work in your life and will continue to do
it.

**Don't be haunted by
the ghosts of a failed marriage.**

Personal Growth and Discussion Questions

1. List some of the personal fears that you have in thinking about building a new relationship.

2. What have you learned about yourself at this stage of your divorce?

3. Describe the person you married the first time and the kind of person you would like to marry in the future.

4. What role is God playing in your life as you think about building a new relationship?

5. My personal growth goal for this week is

TEN

Remarriage—Yours, Mine, and Maybe Our Families'

"When I got married I was looking for an ideal; then it became an ordeal. Now I want a new deal."

Finding a "new deal" in remarriage is not always easy. If divorce has its spectrum of problems and frustrations, remarriage has its own challenges to all who enter in. Many people who find a new relationship that results in marriage seem to feel that things will be just as they were in their previous marriage. The only difference will be the new spouse. It does not take very long to find out that remarriage places a person in a whole new world with added complications to daily routines. A remarriage is not simply a union between two people, as it might have been the first time. It is also a union between two different families, and if both former spouses have remarried, it could well be a union between four different families. It could double your pleasure and quadruple your frustrations.

Working out the intricacies of two- and four-family living takes time, and there are a number of things to consider and think through both prior to and after remarriage.

Pre-remarriage Considerations

The seven pre-remarriage questions that follow are samples of the questions to ask.

1. How many children will be directly involved in the marriage, who will have custody, who will support them, and where will they live? Because we are speaking about unknown situations here, we will not try to answer the questions but merely ask them and let you wrestle with them.

2. How much of the new family's income will go to support the former spouse and children?

3. Where will you live—his house, your house, or a new house? Many hurts are spared when new housing is provided. This avoids anyone being a guest in another person's home.

4. How will the children address their new parents?

5. Where will children who live with former spouses stay when they come for weekends, vacations, or overnight?

6. What about legal adoptions and name changes for the children?

7. How will discipline be handled in the home? Will favoritism be shown to one mate's children over the other's?

These are just a few of the many things that come up when children are involved in remarriage. If children are grown and married, the problems may move to the grandfather/grandmother level. A list of potential problems should be made prior to remarriage and thoroughly discussed. Waiting until the problems occur will not enhance the happiness of a new marriage.

Three things that never seem to be totally resolved in most remarriages are the ongoing relationship with the former spouse, the fair and even treatment of the children on both sides, and the constant strain of stretching the family budget over two households.

From my experience of working with formerly married persons who enter new marriages, the following things will need attention and resolving if the marriage is to be successful.

Who Should You Be Loyal To?

Present spouse? Former spouse? Your own children? Your inherited children? On the surface, the answer might be quite obvious to you. But life is lived out where the little things are faced on an hour-to-hour basis. Loyalties that are clearly thought out may change with new circumstances. If your former spouse were critically ill in another state, would you drop everything and run to his or her bedside? If your new mate exacts severe discipline on your children, will your loyalty be to him or her or to the children? If your children seem to be getting in the way and trying to wreck your new marriage, where will your loyalties be placed?

Parents need to support each other and stand with each other. Many children try to wreck a new marriage by playing one parent against the other. Some might simply want their own parent back and feel very resentful and hostile to the new substitute parent. Spending time talking with the children prior to the marriage will be helpful. Any child will wonder about the role of a new parent coming into the home. Will this person be kind, harsh, loving, mean? They want to know how their lives will be affected by this new relationship. A first family has a chance to grow into things. A second family is thrown into things. Too many times discussions and decisions come after the fact. The time to discuss loyalties on all levels is before they are challenged.

How to Win with Stepchildren

No one can become an instant father or mother overnight. It is going to take time and adjustment on everyone's part. Many new parents simply expect stepchildren to welcome them with open arms and keep living as though nothing had happened. Few children make an easy adjustment, especially if their real parent is close by and in contact with them. The first rule for success as a stepparent is to give the new relationship time to grow and develop.

The second step would be to really work at building that relationship. Your new position in the home may grant you authority, but respect is something you earn. I feel that the responsibility is on the shoulders of the new parent to work at winning the respect and love of the stepchildren. A child may resent a new parent for showing love and affection for his mother or father when little of that love is shown to him. I have known stepparents who have literally ignored their stepchildren and left them entirely up to the natural parent. Few homes will survive this kind of cold treatment.

A third step in winning with stepchildren is to make them feel as important as your own natural children. A love that is shared equally will bring great returns. There are a million ways a stepparent can share and show love. Love always wins.

A fourth step is to realize that you are not a replacement for the other parent. Don't try to be. You are who you are and not a replica of the departed parent. Don't get trapped into playing the role and letting yourself be compared with the absent father or mother. Affirm your own individuality from the beginning and you will gain respect.

How to Adjust to Different Lifestyles

In remarriage, children have to adjust to and compete with different lifestyles. One lifestyle is maintained in the weekday home where they live, while a quite different lifestyle may be lived when they visit their weekend parent. If the weekend parent has not remarried, visitations may be an endless round of entertainment and fun-making. Discipline may be totally abandoned. The return to reality on Sunday evening can be quite traumatic, and it may take several days for the children to adjust to their weekday home.

Separated parents need to work at coordinating lifestyles for the children that will not have great variances in them. If the weekend parent has remarried, an honest effort should be put forth to make the weekend an extension of the week rather than an interference or climax to the child's week. Many parents fail to realize that they put their children on emotional roller coasters by failing to strive for some continuity in schedules, disciplines, entertainments, and acceptance. Too many parents think only of themselves, and the children become an addendum to their lifestyles.

When cooperation is lacking in the other parent to maintain a smooth flow in the children's lifestyle, it would be helpful to explain to the child what is really going on and why. Children can understand many things if time is taken for the explanation. People have a right to live as they choose to live, but only so far as that freedom is not an infringement upon the healthy growth of another person.

How to Treat Your Spouse's Former Mate

In an earlier chapter, we referred to the fact that divorce is unlike death because it leaves the former mate hovering about the fringes of the broken relationship. Prior to a remarriage by one or both parties, there usually is a constant barrage of nit-picking and disagreement on everything under the sun. When one party remarries, the tensions begin to lessen somewhat due to the diversion of having to turn attentions in another direction. When both parties remarry, the tension usually begins to disappear completely as both parties have their time well filled with other things.

It is at this point that healthy relationships can be built with former mates. This may appear to be an ideal to some or something to be avoided by others. The need to have a smooth relationship with a former mate is extremely important if you have children. Emotional wars take a high toll on a person's well-being and stability. The ideal in any divorce situation is to end up having the former mate as a friend. It is easier to live around a friend than an enemy.

A new mate can help you develop a growing relationship with your former spouse by helping you see things objectively. We all need people who act as interpreters and facilitators in our life. They help us explore what is being said and done by seeing that we keep our psychological distance. They can assume the role of sounding board and emotional buffer for us.

A new mate can also develop a hospitable friendship with your former spouse. This will probably happen only if he or she is personally very secure.

We all have to learn in life to work with other people. We cannot always run from those who are difficult. It is doubtful that a high social and friendship level will be desired or reached in former mate remarriage structures. An honest goal would be to have a relationship that is devoid of hostility and open to honest communication as is needed.

If communication is open and honest, positive construction will take place in the lives of the children and parents. It is a high ideal but well worth aiming for.

How to Relate to In-laws, Outlaws, and Other Friends

Some remarriages will cause you to acquire a whole new world of friends and relatives, while others will cause you to lose them. Your family and friends may not agree with your choice and discontinue their relationships with you. Other people will be supportive and continue friendships. A remarriage will place you in a whole new world as far as family and friends are concerned. There is very little you can say or do if people exclude you as a friend or relative. In all likelihood you will win a few and lose a few.

A good guideline here would be to work at keeping the friendships you value and let the other person make the decision. Some remarried persons have a very high level of friendship with former in-laws and relatives. There is no need for those relationships to die simply because of divorce or remarriage. Most of us can use all the friends we can get. If children have had good relationships with grandparents prior to your divorce, they should not be cut off from them. Favorite aunts and uncles should not be severed from friendship because of a divorce.

Some remarrying people want to cut all the old ties and make new ones. People on the fringes of your divorce will hurt for you because of the situation. They do not need to have you hurt them back by cutting off their friendship.

Evaluate the quality of your friendships with your relatives and friends. Keep the ones that are healthy and valuable to everyone. Divorce and remarriage do not have to make you an outlaw.

How to Grow Together

I have shared some thoughts in this chapter about the children, relatives, friends, and former mates. They all make up a part of the world of the remarried. But at the center of that world are the two people who have made new vows and commitments to love, support, honor, and share their lives.

Beginning again in marriage is not easy. It will take more time and patience than you ever dreamed you had. There will be a multitude of little things to be worked out each day. Things you thought you had resolved will keep coming up. You will discover some things you had not discovered prior to the marriage. There will be money problems, children problems, discipline problems, former-mate problems, adjustment problems, legal problems, and personality problems. There will be times when you may wonder what you have gotten into.

After many years of watching people divorce and many choosing to marry again, I have assembled 11 of the most common mistakes men and women make in a second (or third or fourth) marriage. To be forewarned is to be forearmed.

1. One party or the other is really not ready to marry again.

2. The party who is ready pushes the party who is not ready (sometimes out the door, other times down the aisle toward the altar).

3. One party saves the other party through an emotional collision. (I'll take your pain away. I'll marry you.)

4. Dragging your unresolved baggage from a former marriage into a new one. (Remember, check your baggage when you remarry!)

5. An unwillingness to grow and do your own homework. (Homework takes time, and you have to do your own.)

6. Not enough time invested to get to know the entire new family system that is about to become your new family. (Check and see what kind of future relatives have been hidden away in the barn.)

7. No shared dreams. (You can't hitch a ride on someone else's dream.)

8. No shared histories. (In a second [or more] marriage, everyone comes with a history attached.)

9. Too close too soon. (If I push this relationship, I can save time.)

10. Ignoring the problems that arise in another marriage is a sure guarantee of another trip through divorce country.

11. The children are not ready for this. (But if we push them, it will be fine. Wrong! Wrong! Wrong!)

Before You Ever Say "I Do" Again, Think About the Following

1. AIDS test. Smart people do it.

2. Credit check. Really smart people do it.

3. Police check. Really, really smart people do it.

4. Prenuptial agreement. Only those who own nothing should be exempt from this one.

5. Premarital testing. A good psychologist or counselor can do this for you and it's fun.

I will admit that those two lists are scary, but I have been working in this area too long not to be honest with you. You will never do too much homework.

Growing a marriage is never easy, whether it is the first or second or third time around. There are always new lessons to be learned and new loves to share. The need to hang together and maintain a united effort is of extreme importance in a remarriage. There are many things that will bump into your marriage and try to steer it off course. Your commitment to one another needs to be firm and deep. If you think of jumping ship at the first sign of struggle, take a second look at your commitment and priorities.

I saw a little sign once that said, "Things are to be used, people are to be loved." It takes time to grow love. Remarriage is a genuine labor of love, and it doesn't grow and bloom overnight.

Watch out for emotional collisions.
They can be damaging to your future!

Personal Growth and Discussion Questions

1. Finish this statement: The thought of remarriage makes me feel

   Explain your response.

2. Describe how you might feel about loyalties in remarriage.

3. How do you feel about inheriting someone else's children?

4. What would be your greatest fear as a stepparent?

5. Explain how you have kept or lost relatives and friends through your divorce.

6. What three goals would you set for yourself in a remarriage?

7. My personal growth goal for this week is

ELEVEN

How to Keep the Scales of Justice from Tilting

"Why do I need an attorney?"

Divorce is the death of a marriage and is usually surrounded by a cast of players that includes the husband and wife as combatants, the children as the mourners, and the lawyers as the funeral directors.

Lawyers are often maligned for the role they play in the divorce cases in our society. Some look upon them as eager vultures in search of big fees. Others look to them as friends and guides in this strange land called divorce country. They know the bends in the road, the potholes, the construction areas, the danger zones, the dead ends. They are often thrust into the roles of social worker, counselor, therapist, priest, and doctor. A good lawyer will not forget to put his humanity and love for people alongside his law books and court presentations.

One of the first questions I ask a person who announces they are contemplating or are in the process of divorce is, "Have you obtained an attorney and consulted with him or her?" I am amazed at how many people leave this decision up to someone else or just don't think of it at all. Many who do not want a divorce respond by saying, "Why do I need an attorney?"

One of the most important things to remember, whether you want the divorce or not, is to get an attorney right away! A good divorce attorney can make a world of difference in helping you walk through all the legal implications of divorce.

I meet people every day who were tricked, conned, and hoodwinked into losing literally everything in their divorce because they did not secure a good attorney in time. If one mate has a competent attorney and the other does not, it may mean the difference between a good settlement and a bad one.

Where Do You Find a Good Attorney?

Most attorneys come through personal recommendation of friends or relatives. They should not come through leafing through the yellow pages of your telephone book. A telephone call to the local bar association can often be beneficial in helping you find a lawyer who specializes in divorce cases. You do need an attorney who specializes in family law rather than one who does corporate law and handles two or three divorces a year for friends. The laws regarding divorce in many states are changing rapidly, and you do need an attorney who keeps up with those changes and understands their impact on you, the client. A good question of inquiry to an attorney would be, "What percentage of your cases each year deal with divorce?" If the percentage is high, it could indicate that the attorney specializes in this area. Don't be afraid to ask questions. Find out what you need to know before you hire legal counsel.

Some Helpful Hints from an Attorney

I have asked an attorney friend of mine who specializes in divorce proceedings to share some of his wisdom with you. Here are his suggestions:

1. Exhaust all reasonable joint efforts in seeking competent family counseling before seeking divorce.

    a. Singular efforts of one spouse seldom result in joint insight into the problems and solutions that can keep a marriage together.

    b. Carefully select a counselor through trusted sources of referral or recommendation.

    c. Approach all counseling with an open mind. At worst you might get a new look at "the real you."

2. If there is a basis to believe one party will abscond with or dissipate liquid assets (joint bank accounts, etc.), freeze these assets (by removal to singular bank accounts, etc.).

    a. This is not considered improper. Such action simply preserves the estate for future disposition (payment of debts, equal division of community property, attorney fees, etc.)

    b. No unfair advantage is gained. The court can require you to account for these assets at a later date, which you should be able and willing to do.

3. Avoid the "do-it-yourself divorce" (now called "dissolution" in California) unless there are little or no assets and no issues of child or spousal support (alimony).

4. Discussions of settlements with your spouse's attorney may be acceptable, but never enter into any final agreement until you at least consult with counsel of your own choosing.

    a. Conserving attorney's fees is commendable, but not at the cost of your unending regret.

b. Do not be lulled into the belief that one attorney can represent both parties. If in doubt, ask the attorney who his client really is.

5. If litigation ensues, select your attorney carefully. Again, seek your attorney through a trusted source of referral. Changing horses in midstream can be expensive.

6. Personally evaluate your attorney. (Oh yes, you can!)

a. Ask him pointed questions (evaluate the directness and logic of his answers):
— Length of time in practice
— Experience in the field of family law
— Anticipated fees and costs
— How he intends to approach his task

b. Do not always expect concrete, definitive answers at the first conference, as they are seldom possible. In fact, be wary of "guarantees."

c. Have a firm understanding with him. Do you feel you have a rapport?

7. Have a firm understanding with your attorney as to his fees from the outset.

a. It is your right to know. (When is the last time you made a major purchase without first asking the price?)

b. Beware of the attorney who is resentful of questions about his fees. (You can't afford him, in more ways than you know.)

8. Feel free at all times to frankly discuss the problems and to ask questions of your attorney.

a. Don't complain about not getting answers if you never asked.

b. Never lie to your attorney (or doctor or minister).

c. Listen to and act on his advice. That's what you are paying for.

9. Communicate your fears and desires to your attorney. Although results cannot be guaranteed, it is only in this fashion that your attorney can attempt to get the desired results in the end.

10. Live with the results. Vindictiveness leads to destruction. Learn from yesterday and prepare for tomorrow. Remember, you can always go back to court on key issues at a later date if you need to. It may be costly, but the issues of child and spousal support, visitation, and custody can change in the months and years after your divorce.

What About Mediation?

Though it has been around the court systems in most states since the 1970s, mediation is gaining in recognition and use across the country. Many family therapists call mediation the safe and sane and less hostile route through divorce country.

Many family law attorneys have been specially trained to do mediation work along with family counselors. Those trained in the skills of mediation hope that the communications tools learned through mediation in divorce will minimize a couple's emotional and financial losses during and after a divorce.

Gary J. Friedman, attorney and mediator, is the author of *A Guide to Divorce Mediation: How to Reach a Fair and Legal Settlement at a Fraction of the Cost* (Workman Publishing). He identifies four criteria for successful mediation in his book. They are:

1. Motivation to mediate. Mediation will undoubtedly fail if one of you feels forced into it.
2. Self-responsibility. You must understand your own situation and set your own priorities.

3. Willingness to disagree. You must be able to stand up for yourself and refuse a settlement that won't let you move ahead with your life.

4. Willingness to agree. Mediation won't work if you don't strive for an agreement.

You can find a trained mediator by contacting your county family or domestic relations court, calling a counseling service, or checking the internet.

Mediation can save you thousands of dollars in lawyer and court costs. It can reduce the tension, anger, and revenge many seek when a marriage ends in divorce. Mediation also allows you a greater degree of self-responsibility in solving the many problems that divorce creates. Remember, it only works if both parties are willing.

Practical Observations

1. Remember that legal proceedings take time. Courts have great backlogs of cases. Yours is not the only one before them. Many divorce proceedings can go on for several years, depending upon the involvements.

2. Don't call your lawyer every day about the irrelevant and mundane things that you are going through. His work is legal. A good counselor or therapist can help you with the nonlegal issues.

3. Don't sign any papers or make any agreements with a former spouse without consulting your lawyer.

4. Let your lawyer speak for you in legal matters.

5. Remember that in the heat of personal emotional conflict in divorce, the coolest head on your side may be your attorney. Listen to his wisdom and clear thinking.

6. Divorce laws in our country are changing rapidly. They vary from state to state. Don't assume that something you heard from another state is true in yours.

7. Don't take legal advice from your friends who have gone through a divorce. Every situation is unique in itself and there are too many variables to assume that you can do what someone else did or that your end results will be the same as theirs.

8. Be wary of the rash of "do-it-yourself divorce kits" available in most bookstores. The "you-do-it" kits are fine if you have no property, no possessions, no children, no money, and are moving to an island in the Pacific. In today's world, that's a very small group.

9. A number of divorce clinics are springing up around the country. They generally offer paralegal assistance and all the forms you need to file for a divorce. They will walk you through all your paperwork and help you file everything without the assistance of an attorney or the fees that come attached to that attorney. Some people have found these services satisfying and money-saving. Others have been frustrated with employees who may not know what they are talking about. If you choose this route, get solid recommendations from previous clients along with a list of the right people to see if you go there.

10. We have reached the era where most states now have joint property and joint custody laws. Both of these were started with good intentions in mind from our legal system. They both simply mean that everything is to be divided equally where possessions are concerned and equal responsibility for the children after divorce is the goal. Sometimes this works well. At other times it doesn't.

The legal involvements of divorce are seldom easy. Someone has said that anyone experiencing divorce needs three things: a good friend, a good attorney, and God.

Personal Growth and Group Discussion Questions

1. Did you have your own attorney during your divorce?

2. What kind of job did he or she do in your behalf?

3. Do you feel you received fair treatment in the legal aspects of your divorce settlement?

4. Describe what you learned from the legal aspects of your divorce.

5. How would you change any of the current divorce laws in your state?

6. Were your legal settlements simple or complex? Explain if you can, without being too personal.

7. My personal growth goal for this week is

TWELVE

Get a Life... Yours!

---

*"If you don't know who you are, you
won't know where you are going."*

As I talk with hundreds of people each year who are processing their divorce, I hear many expressing confusion about their identity (who they are now) and their direction (where they are now going). Too many have either buried their identity in a past marriage or had a controlling spouse who robbed them of their identity. When they become single again, their biggest struggle is finding out who they are at this moment in their life.

Not knowing who you are is bad enough. Not knowing your direction in life is even worse. Many men and women, while married, had their daily plans and life direction spelled out by their spouse. They simply followed orders and really did not have to spend much time wondering about where they were personally or collectively headed. After a divorce they quickly discover that no one is calling the signals in their life any longer and the responsibility is now up to them.

There are four basic questions that you can use as a guide to getting your life back on track after a divorce. I suggest you divide a sheet of blank paper into four blocks. Write one of

131

these questions at the top of each block: Who am I now? Where am I going? How will I get there? Who will help me? This is no easy homework assignment. You may have to spend some significant hours working on your responses. The end result will be the beginning of a game plan for some of the rest of your life.

You will notice that the third and fourth questions will bring a cast of supporting players into your life. You are not intended to be a lone ranger and operate without the help of others. God uses people to help us reach our goals and attain our dreams.

Let me raise a small caution flag right here. Too many men and women who have lost their identity and direction as a result of divorce quickly try to find another person who will restore that to their life. A second marriage ensues and they slip back into their former track, never really discovering anything about themselves.

One of the basic reasons we emphasize the two- to three-year recovery period is to enable people to discover who they really are, where they want to go in life, who will help them get there, and what means or routes they must take on that journey. Those who work on this form of rebuilding will discover that when they marry again, they will marry from strength and not from weakness. They will also marry someone who has a strong sense of purpose, direction, and identity.

Building a new life after divorce means setting some goals that can be reached and celebrated. Some of them need to be short-term so that victory is attainable and affirmation can be restored to the person who has lost self-worth and a sense of productivity.

The following goals for getting a new life after divorce will demand time and energy from those who attempt to follow them. It is a long-term plan and not intended to be microwaved in your mind and quickly filed under Done That. Work on these goals by yourself and then talk them through with trusted friends who can give you some accountability. Remember, no accountability usually means no completion. No completion means you stay where you are.

Relational Goals

We said earlier that divorce can cause you to lose a great many friends you had when you were married. As they disappear, you need to build a new friendship scaffolding around your life. You can start by asking past friends to remain friends with you in this new part of your life. Some will. Some will not. You can assess your friendship needs by answering this question: "Who do I need in my life relationally as a part of an ongoing support system that will remain in place no matter what might happen to me in the future?" One good answer might be, "I need more fun people in my life. My past friends were too serious."

A second question might involve evaluating the friends that remain in your life. Are some of them toxic while other are nourishing? Are some depressing while others are encouraging? Are some only there in good times and exit when you really need them? I think you get the idea.

A good relational goal might be to find a dynamic and nurturing singles' group somewhere in your community. Even though many jokes are made about singles' groups, there are many around filled with quality people just like you. Remember, we often make our best friends when we are in the midst of our biggest struggles.

I am often asked, "Is it okay to have a relational goal of one day finding the right person and remarrying?" Yes! And don't be afraid to put it on your long-term list of goals if that is what you desire. Few divorcing people can bear the thought of ever remarrying, but just wait a few years. Once the anger, pain, rejection, hurt, and chaos of divorce is past and you are feeling good about yourself and your future, the possibility of remarriage may appear on the horizon in your life.

Divorce always changes relationships in the family experiencing its impact. It also changes relationships with people in your church, career, and community. Relational losses are inevitable. Relational rebuilding is a mandate. Set some goals and remember the words of good old Charlie Brown: "I need all the friends I can get!"

Personal Goals

Personal goals are goals you set for yourself that are not contingent upon anyone else. You know if you succeed and you also know if you fail. An everyday example of a personal goal is losing weight. We all talk about it and inform our friends that we will start tomorrow, next week, or next year. No one ever seems to ask, "How is your diet going?" We take refuge in the fact that we can always start and if it ends, we can start all over.

In the Olympics, you will hear the term "personal best." It means that athletes have set personal goals to do better than they have in the past in their sport. Each time they set a new time or record, that becomes their standard or personal best. They are really competing against themselves. If their best time is better than anyone else's, they have a good shot at winning their event when it takes place.

Personal goals are often the hardest to accomplish. No one is cheering on the sidelines as you struggle toward your goal. No one may even be cheering for you when you attain it. I remember when the first copy of a new book I had written appeared in my mailbox. I wanted to run up and down the street and tell my neighbors and the whole community that I had written a new book. The reality was that hardly anyone knew I was writing it, and they could have cared less that it was now published and in the bookstores.

If you were to make a short list right now of five very personal goals for yourself, what would they be? How badly do you want to attain them, and how will they impact your life when accomplished?

Many people have spent years of their life accomplishing other people's goals. Some have paid dearly for that prize when the other person received it. Divorce, more than any other life event, forces you to take aim at a few targets of your own selection. What will they be for you?

Vocational Goals

One of the first things we ask a new acquaintance after "Where do you live?" is "What do you do?" The question doesn't mean, "What do you do at different times of the day?" We want to know what their vocation is and where they work in the community. It tells us a lot about a person without asking further questions.

One of the questions we seldom ask is, "Why do you do that?" (after their response to "What do you do?"). I have asked that question a few times only to hear responses like "I don't have any idea," or "This is what I was trained for," or "This is what everyone in our family does."

Vocations are important to all of us. They give our life purpose and meaning. Hopefully they also give us an annual income. When we change them or lose them, confusion and chaos can ensue.

Very few people lose vocations as a result of divorce (clergymen excepted). Many people during and after the divorce experience choose to change jobs or even vocations. Some discover that they were never happy with their vocational choice and now can choose to do something different with their lives. Others who have never had a vocation now need one for financial reasons.

A vocation comes about by training, calling, giftedness, default, choice, or change. There are several questions I ask people when we talk about setting new vocational goals.

1. Why are you doing what you are doing vocationally?
2. Is it the best use of your gifts, talents, and abilities?
3. Does it cause you more happiness than unhappiness?
4. Does it give you a sense of fulfillment at the end of the day?
5. Do you feel this is what God would have you do?

Getting a new life for yourself may mean vocational change. What goals do you need to set in this area as you rebuild?

Spiritual Goals

The crisis of divorce can pull you toward God or it can drive you away from God. If you prayed to God that your divorce would not happen and it still did, you can get mad at God and toss in the towel on your spiritual life. If you were not very spiritual before your divorce, you can find yourself reaching out to God for the help you need to survive the experience. If you had a spiritual life before your divorce and you have grown stronger spiritually through your divorce, you have discovered that truth from Scripture that says, "I can do all things through [Christ] who strengthens me" (Philippians 4:13).

Divorce impacts your life spiritually. It can weaken you or it can strengthen you. It can destroy your Christian community or it can draw that community closer to you. It can drive you to deepening your walk with God or it can drive you to abandoning your walk with God.

Setting spiritual goals starts when you ask yourself where you are spiritually and where you would like to be spiritually a year from now, six months from now, or even next week. It can present new challenges for spiritual growth and developing a closer walk with God.

Here are a few practical goals that you can set in the spiritual area that will help you grow.

1. Read books that will help you grow spiritually.
2. If you don't have one, find a Christian fellowship that will love and support you.
3. Spend some quiet minutes each day with God in reflection, prayer, and worship.
4. Plan a solitary spiritual retreat with just you and God away from all the daily activity and noise in your life. Twenty-four hours is good for a start.
5. Find a couple of spiritual friends who will pray for you and support you.

These are only a few goals…you can add more of your own.

Financial Goals

Divorces cost a lot of money. Few people from my experience come out the other side with more than spare change and a few postage stamps. Many end up in bankruptcy and financial ruin with a bad credit rating and a mountain of bills and attorney fees to pay. Houses are sold and apartments rented. Personal belongings are sold or divided up. More than a few men and women have told me that their sole goal was to just keep breathing and pay the bills.

Getting a new life financially takes time and often some outside help. Debt counseling, financial planning, and budget-making are small parts of setting new financial goals. They become operative by asking the questions, "Where am I financially now and where do I want to be financially one, three, or five years from today?" and "What is my plan to get there?"

There are many new books on the market that can assist in helping you stabilize and organize your finances. Banks have people that will assist you in budgeting and planning financially. The bottom line is simple. When you need some help in this area, ask for it, find it, and utilize it.

Educational Goals

Margaret was fearful of going back to school. She dreaded that first day of class at the local community college. She went at the very last minute and took the last seat still empty in the classroom. She only breathed a sigh of relief after she looked around the room at the other 34 people present and realized over 80 percent were at least her age or older. They were all facing the growth process of re-education.

Whether you have been unemployed prior to your divorce or your company is sending you back to school for further education, you will be one among many setting new educational goals for your life. It may mean working for a completed college education you abandoned many years earlier or simply adding credentials that will keep advancement coming in your vocation.

Setting educational goals involves asking yourself the question, "What kind of education do I need that will equip me to reach my vocational goals?" "How long will it take?" and "How will I pay for it?" are other questions. Many returning students today have discovered that their academic brain still works and they can bring home top grades.

Many community colleges offer skill and interest testing today if you don't know what courses to take or what career to pursue. Most of it is free and just involves your taking the time and risk.

Remember, only people who quit growing don't have to do their homework!

Family Goals

If you are divorced and have children, you are still a family. If your children still live at home after a divorce, life will go on and follow routines, responsibilities, and regimens. You will quickly discover that being a single parent is a lot tougher than being part of a two-parent household. For single parents, it's either too little or too much of everything.

Setting goals for your family involves every member of your family. You are still a team, and a team works together. Your first goal may be survival. After a while, others will pop up. Sharing family celebrations, vacations, school events, etc., are only a few. What are some goals you would like to see your family establish? Who will participate and what's the cost of attaining these goals? Which family goals can you carry over from before the divorce? Which ones need to change? How will new goals impact family members?

Remember, you don't divorce your family. Even if you are the noncustodial parent, you need to be a part of setting family goals.

Health Goals

Divorce can be a disease that destroys your health and physical being. Many people in an emotional crisis do not think of their health. They spend consummate hours thinking about their problem and the "what ifs" and "if I'd onlys." What impacts your mind can eventually impact your body unless you cognitively work to prevent it. I watch people every day who lose hope, lose weight, fall into depression, and end up not caring what happens in their lives. When your emotional side collapses, it is often followed by physical problems. You can soon end up in the local psychiatric ward of your favorite hospital.

Some good goals here would be:

1. Get a physical checkup first. Find out if everything is working properly.
2. Get into a daily physical exercise program at the YMCA or at a local gym or class.
3. Start to eat right. Stay away from fast foods and the snack monster.
4. Find a sport you can participate in that gives you a good workout.
5. Hang out with people who care about their bodies and take care of them.
6. Remember, your body is a temple that God has entrusted to you. Make it a good place for Him to inhabit. You are His creative work.

Sexual Goals

A tough question that comes up in most divorce-recovery seminars in our small-group discussion times is, "How do you handle your sexuality after a divorce?" That's a veiled way of asking, "Is it okay to have a sexual relationship with the opposite sex if you are not married to them?" Perhaps what many people are asking is, "Tell me if it is right or wrong and I will go and do what you say."

For a Christian man or woman, the question is never, "What can I do or not do?" The real question is, "What would God have me do and what does His Word say about this particular thing?" Our real wrestling match on the serious issues of life is not with the opinions of others but with God and His desire for our lives. That might prompt us to conclude that if one is not a Christian, he or she can do whatever they want, anytime, anywhere, as long as it is within the law. If one is a Christian then the question is, "God, what would You have me to do?"

The Christian standard of human sexuality almost disappeared in the last part of the twentieth century. The secular message that says, "If it feels good, do it" has slipped into our logic and reasoning even in the Christian community.

Having and exploring some goals in this area is a good beginning to getting a handle on how you will deal with your sexuality as a single-again person. A few good goals might be:

1. What does the Bible really say about this?
2. Does anyone else struggle with this problem like I do?
3. What resources can I read that will help me?
4. How can I let other people know what my standards are?
5. How can I deal with those people who have different standards?

If you choose to search out what Scripture says, you might start with 1 Corinthians 10:31 and 1 Corinthians 6:12-20.

You may end up by simply stating, "My goal is to have a goal in the sexual area and not allow anything to take that goal away." Remember, for the Christian, it's not what other people think. It is what God says.

Emotional Goals

If I asked you today how you were doing emotionally, what would you say? Good! Awful! Basket case! Hanging on! Dying on the vine! Growing!

Living in divorce country consists of a daily series of ups and downs. It could aptly be described as a roller coaster ride with the most expensive fare you have ever paid. On bad days, you wonder if you will ever get off and resume normal living (whatever that means).

Emotions are like little hooks that reach out and snag you when you least expect them. They can bring you down when you thought you were really on the way up.

The first year of divorce could be described as "crazy time" emotionally. The second year involves emotional adjustment. Along about year three, emotional balance begins to be the norm. Most divorcing men and women that I meet want to jump from month one to year three. Emotions are expressed by feelings, and we have to process them as they occur. Owning one's feelings is part of good growth.

Setting some emotional goals starts by assessing where you are today emotionally. There is your opinion, your friends' opinions, your families' opinions, and your therapists' opinions. If you ask all four groups, you should get a good reading.

Once you assess where you are, you decide where you want to be down the road. There is usually a price tag in reaching emotional goals. The process can be painful before you feel any gain.

One lady recently summed up her emotional goal for me. She said "I just want to stop crying and feeling miserable all the time." Good goal. It is achievable by working at it.

Emotions that are expressed need good sounding boards. Understanding and caring friends can be that for you if you will allow it.

This is only a short list of goals as you rebuild your life. You can add any others you think of to the list. They all spell out growth for your life and can best be expressed in the following words from an unknown author:

> *Growth is betrayal of arrangements that were...*
> *Growth is change that is threatening*
> *as well as promising...*
> *Growth is denial of something and*
> *affirmation of something else...*
> *Growth is dangerous and glorious insecurity.*

It is time for you to get a life. Yours!

Personal Growth and Discussion Questions

1. Share with your group your response to the questions: Who am I now? Where am I going? How will I get there? and Who will help me?

2. Of the ten goals listed in this chapter, what appears to be most difficult for you and why? Easiest and why?

3. As you work on rebuilding your life, describe what you would like the finished "you" to look like.

4. Finish this statement: "The thing I am most excited about now as I think about rebuilding my life is…"

THIRTEEN

The Most Frequently Asked Questions About Divorce

I see it written on the faces of men and women in every divorce-recovery workshop that I conduct. It is the ultimate question that everyone asks when confronted with a life-threatening crisis: "Will I survive this experience, and if I do, what kind of condition will I be in when the event is behind me?"

If I had not worked in the divorce-recovery field for so many years, I doubt that I would be able to answer this question. After working with thousands of men and women of all ages as well as children young and old, I can assure you the reader that your chances of surviving your divorce are excellent and that you will be in wonderful condition down the road if you choose to grow through your experience.

Between survival and growth, you will process a number of questions. Some of your questions will undoubtedly be among those that follow. Since answers often have a way of narrowing your options, I would like to offer my responses to the following questions as suggestions from the edge of my experience.

1. *How long am I going to feel this pain?*

Emotional pain is far more difficult to resolve than physical pain. There are no pills to take, only a process to struggle through. Elisabeth Kübler-Ross talks about the pain of dying as a process. Her five stages are denial, anger, bargaining, depression, and acceptance. Divorce is the death of a relationship. For most people, processing those stages usually takes from a year to 18 months. When personal growth begins to take over the pain, the healing process becomes more evident. Remember, it is normal to own and process your pain.

2. *Do men and women who have an "affair" and leave their spouses ever come back?*

Those that do are very few in number. When a person has an affair, all their energies are directed to the new person in their life. Seldom are any energies extended to repairing the broken relationship, regardless of the things that led up to the relational breakdown. Remember, the doorway back after any affair is through a counselor's office. The hurdles then to conquer are forgiveness and renewed trust.

3. *What is the best way to help your children through your divorce?*

The greatest gifts a parent can give to a child during divorce are love and time. Children often feel rejected by one parent or the other and desperately need to still know they are loved. Time for fun and time for talking will amplify the message of love to your children.

There are also many children's workshops available to help them process their parents' divorce. Check with local churches, community colleges, or counseling centers and get your children involved.

4. *When can I safely start dating again?*

The greatest danger in divorce country is to try to remove the pain of your divorce by having an emotional collision with another man or woman. Some return to dating before their divorce is even finalized with the intent of proving to their former spouse that they can catch a "replacement" and flaunt their success. Rejection is seldom solved with a replacement. You need to be whole, healed, and happy with yourself before you ever consider dating. Remember, you could end up married to your next date! Are you really ready for that? My suggestion is wait 18–24 months after your divorce is finalized.

5. *How do you deal with your in-laws during and after a divorce?*

Carefully! Many in-laws tend to take the side of their son or daughter regardless of the wanton crimes the person has committed against you. Once in a while, insightful in-laws will take your side and condemn their own child.

Since your in-laws are your children's grandparents (if you have children), those relationships should stay intact after a divorce. In-laws are often in a deeper quandary than you are and need time and talking to work out an amicable, ongoing relationship. Don't make them choose sides. They did not cause the divorce. Don't be afraid to tell them you love them and still want and need them in your life.

6. *Is there any easy or better way to deal with holidays and special events when you enter divorce country?*

Facing those special events in the first year of your divorce is most difficult. You find yourself remembering happier times and want those times back. You will want to run away and hide until the event is over. Thanksgiving, Christmas, birthdays, and anniversaries are often the most difficult. The biggest struggle is usually who gets the children for the longest amount of time and who treated them best when they had them.

If you can communicate with your former spouse, try to get all the plans set well in advance of the event. If you are the one alone for a time, fill that time with other friends and activities so that you won't feel abandoned.

Children are often the victims of the holiday tug-of-war. Talk with them about their desires and wishes. Hear what they feel before adult decisions are made. And above all, be fair!

7. *If it takes two to three years to rebuild your life after divorce, what do you do during those years?*

Take some time to lay out a personal growth plan for yourself. Include major changes you would like to make as well as setting some goals to be attained. A good starting point is to take the ten types of goals from the "Get a Life...Yours!" chapter and start thinking and praying about what you would like to achieve in those areas. Remember, if you don't come up with a plan, you won't have a purpose to rebuild your life. Get some help from people outside of your everyday life. They can often be more objective than you can. Remember, rebuilding takes time. Be kind and give yourself the gift of time.

8. *Does God ever forgive divorced people?*

Christians generally have a hard time with divorce. They have been taught for years that divorce is wrong, and now this wrong-of-all-wrongs has happened to them. Many feel they will forever be condemned by God and never be forgiven even if the divorce wasn't initiated by them.

The good news is that God is in the forgiveness business. Matthew 6:14 (NIV) says, "For if you forgive men when they sin against you, your heavenly Father will also forgive you." This is only one of the many verses in the Bible that speak about forgiveness. There are numerous others that will help you understand that divorce is not the unforgivable sin, even though other Christians might try to tell you it is.

When God forgives us, He puts the forgiven deed out of His sight. Reread the forgiveness chapter (chapter 8) in this book a few times until you absorb its message.

A healthy and growing Christian in the land beyond divorce is a forgiven Christian.

9. What do you do when you are in a divorce and your church rejects you?

Find a new church home fast! Divorce, in and of itself, is a rejection. When a church adds more rejection to what you already feel, it can send you into deep despair. Rejection is never solved by more rejection. It is resolved in part by having those around you accept you…even when you are going through a divorce.

Those who should love you most when you hurt can often hurt you the most when you need to be loved. There are many churches that will open their arms to those in pain and be about the business of bringing hope and healing into your life. It is always hard to leave a place you have known as "home" after many years. It will be harder to stay and absorb the condemnations and rejections. If you are in a church that loves and guides you through your divorce, let them know you appreciate that love and help.

10. What is the best way to tell your children about your divorce?

Too often, the children are never told much of anything regarding the divorce. They pick up bits and pieces and arrive at their own conclusions. Their struggles are often absorbed by their peer group, while their parents focus on their own survival.

There is no easy way to talk about divorce to one's children. Emotions and feelings run high. Anger can trigger misunderstanding and denial. A family talk can turn into a family tragedy.

Children need to hear from both parents, whether in separate meetings or together. Children should be talked with collectively and individually. If you need help, have your pastor or a counselor assist you. Remember, your children need to hear from YOU about what is going on…not from the neighbors.

11. *What about moving to another city or state after a divorce?*

Divorce often keeps you living at the burial site of your marriage. The primary reasons are children, job, support systems, and family ties. If you have none of the above where you have been living prior to divorce, starting over in a new place can be helpful. If you have children, moving is virtually impossible because the courts recognize the need for the other parent to be physically present in your children's lives. And the children have that same right. Moving with children usually demands the other parent's permission. We all need fresh starts and new beginnings after a crisis. It may mean that you can only move across town rather than across the country.

12. *How do you handle the emotional mood swings in divorce?*

Gently! You will have days when the bottom drops out of your life and you feel hopeless. You will have other days when you feel you are getting it together and things are going well. Ups and downs are a given in divorce country. Mood swings can be triggered by a phone call, a memory, an old photograph, or a pile of unpaid bills.

Feelings are neither right nor wrong. You can express them or repress them. Owning your feelings and identifying what triggers them is important to your growth. Find trusted friends to talk through your feelings with. You cannot deny how you really feel for very long. Stay in touch with what's going on inside of you and know that human feelings are a gift of God that makes us unique.

13. *What should your attitude be toward the "affair" person that you feel ruined your marriage?*

You should not buy a gun and try to kill them, and you certainly should not have them over for Sunday brunch! Don't allow them to become a major player in your life from either a destructive or constructive point of view. In spite of what you might believe, they did not cause your divorce. Your former spouse did.

The really tough thing is that your former spouse might marry this person, and he or she would become a stepparent to your children. Your children might eventually like them and enjoy their company. And it's not fair!

14. *Do you really need a support group during and after your divorce?*

Yes! Yes! Yes! There is a certain type of security when you are with fellow strugglers. You can be honest, blunt, expressive, caring, and growing when you are with kindred spirits who have been where you are. There is no posturing, no hiding, and no lying. Every inch of growth that takes place in the life of a fellow support-group member will cause you to cheer and allow you to know that if they can do it, you can also. A support group is a safe haven for broken people and brings hope that together you can face any obstacles in divorce country.

Every community has divorce support groups. Don't stop until you find one.

15. *When is it important to get some professional counseling during divorce?*

When everything piles up and your circuits are on overload and you wonder if you can survive another day, it's time to ask for help in a personalized form. Divorce often triggers unresolved baggage from yesterday in your life. Divorce may only be a door opener to all the years of denial and unresolved problems from childhood, family systems disorders, or personality struggles that seem to worsen as you grow older.

It is never too late to reach out for help and begin a rebuilding process in your life. Listen to your friends, listen to your own heart, and listen to God. There are many competent Christian therapists who can help you deal with struggles past and present.

16. *If you pray hard enough and really believe, will God restore your marriage?*

You will meet some folks who believe this. Usually they are all still married. The struggle here is that the other person you might still want to be married to has made a bad choice in leaving you, but you now have to live out his or her bad choice. God doesn't make people do things. He give them choices. God also doesn't do things on our commands. If He did, we could eliminate all the problems in the world very quickly.

Always remember, it takes two people to restore a marriage. You can pray and you can believe. Christians should do both. They also are often forced to live out someone else's decision.

17. What do you do when your former spouse manipulates your children and uses them against you?

Don't play the same game! That's hard because there is always the desire to fight fire with fire. The bad part is the children become the victims once again. Eventually they can end up hating both parents as they get older. There are many different forms of manipulation and control. Call them what they are and resist getting trapped into those games. No one wins in the long run. Children eventually grow up, become wiser, and can see how they were used.

18. Is there ever a time when a parent should fight for full custody of a child?

Yes, but you have to decide if the victory is worth the cost of the battle. Some parents do it on a whim as a means of revenge and control. The emotions of the children are seldom considered. They become a prize to be won.

You will usually have to prove in court that the other parent is unfit and the children will do better without them. Joint custody is an attempt by our legal system to do away with custody battles. In good circumstances, parenting should be shared even after a divorce. Children still need a mom and a dad. The exception would be where it can be proved that being with the other parent is detrimental to the growth and health of the child.

Remember, custody battles can cost a small fortune.

19. What is the most common mistake divorcing people tend to make?

There really are several from my observation. One would be spending too much time and energy trying to get even with the former spouse. You never win because revenge robs you of energy you need to devote to rebuilding your life. Another would be not accepting the reality that a divorce is happening to you. The sooner you accept the reality, the sooner you start rebuilding your life. A final biggie would be finding a replacement for your former spouse and quickly marrying again. Remember, a greater percentage of second marriages fail than first marriages.

20. *Is grieving a part of the divorce process?*

Definitely! Divorce is a close second to losing a mate by death. The big difference is that in a divorce the person is still alive. You still see them and feel that you will grieve their loss forever. Grief takes time and we all handle it differently. Don't be afraid to declare a "mourning time" for yourself. When it's over, start moving on with your life.

You will cry, you will hide away, and you will feel terrible. Healthy mourning is a process precipitated by loss. Everyone will go through it differently, but everyone will go through it!

21. *How do you keep from being emotionally vulnerable?*

Know your strengths and weaknesses and don't allow yourself to get caught in places and with people who will take advantage of you. Loneliness is often the scourge of divorced people. Some will look for anyone to fill the human gaps in their life and make their loneliness disappear. Remember, pain always makes you vulnerable to rescuers and relational messiahs.

22. *What do you do when your spouse wants to save money by using his or her attorney for both of you?*

Smile knowingly and race out to hire your own attorney. An attorney can legally only represent one person and look out for their best interests. If it's your spouse's attorney, it won't be your best interests. It will cost you more, but you will come out far better in the long run with your own attorney.

23. *What's the best way to deal with rejection?*

Work on building your own self-worth, self-esteem, and self-value. You can't get it from other people. If you try, it will vanish the moment they leave you, and you will be headed for pity city.

We all live with rejection. It is a staple in life's diet. Know that you are loved and accepted by God. Self-esteem for the Christian starts there. Once that is your foundation, you can never be destroyed by others' rejection.

24. *Do you ever get over the bitterness you feel in divorce?*

Yes, if you make it one of your goals. You can stay bitter for years, complain that life is not fair, and never get better. The seeds of bitterness come from the anger we feel when other people have taken advantage of us. We usually are mad at those who caused our bitterness and mad at ourselves for allowing it to happen.

When you begin to do positive, growth-producing things for yourself, you are on the road to healing your bitter spirit.

25. *How do you know if you are doing okay in your journey through divorce country?*

We all need a reality check periodically. Those closest to us can help with that by giving their input. The best friends are honest friends who can speak the truth in love. After you talk with your friends, ask yourself some hard questions and do a "gut" check. There is a process of "letting go" that we spoke about earlier in this book. You have to file the past, live one day at a time in the present, and start setting some goals for your future.

It takes time to grow through a divorce. Be willing to celebrate the moments when you recognize that you are doing better and rebuilding your life one day at a time.

FOURTEEN

How to Help Others Grow Through Divorce

*"It seems like everyone I meet
is getting divorced."*

Depending on what statistics you believe, the divorce rate is either going up or coming down. There is no one reason for the great number of divorces in our society. Every divorce is different and every set of circumstances has its own variables.

We are living in an age of dramatic cultural changes. Traditions, trends, styles, feelings, and attitudes seem to change each time the daily newspaper is published. Values that were held sacred and ideal seem to have vanished into history. Our mobile way of life in both career and daily lifestyle has caused a rootlessness in our families. The concept of a "use and discard" society has crept into the feelings we have about people. A person is used and replaced without much thought of how he or she will be affected. People are discarded in industry and in marriage with about as much concern as we have in throwing our pop bottles in the garbage. Our "people attitudes" become confused with our "merchandising attitudes." If something or someone doesn't work, we throw it away and get a new one. New freedoms and feelings brought about by the women's movement have had a dramatic influence on our changing culture. Man's quest to get in touch with himself and raise his own consciousness level has dramatically influenced contemporary attitudes on many things. However, people will continue to marry and divorce for whatever reasons they can think up.

In a recent conversation, a person said, "It seems like everyone I meet is getting divorced." Somehow when we go through crises in our life, we become very aware of other people around us who are experiencing the same thing. It is easy to attract those who can commiserate with you in your dilemma. It happens if you break your leg, wreck your car, lose your appendix, or leave your marriage. Experience is valuable and it teaches us many things. One of the good things about it is that we can share what we learn with others. After growing through your own divorce, you will have something very valuable to pass along to other people. Here are several guidelines that will enable you to help others who are getting divorced.

Don't Judge

When two people decide to divorce, it usually sets the stage for battle lines to be drawn among the immediate family and friends. People will choose the team they want to support and then begin the process of pronouncing judgments on the other party. Families and friendships are torn to shreds because people refuse to remain neutral and try to be a friend to both divorcing parties. Sometimes people are pushed into taking sides by the separating people themselves. They might not be granted the privilege of neutrality.

In every divorce there are endless entanglements that outsiders should seek to avoid. Express to both divorcing parties that you appreciate each of them as persons and your friendship with them is not based upon their personal performance with each other. Ask them to let you remain neutral and continue your friendship with each as you choose. When family or friends try to induce you to take sides, tell them you are not qualified to be either lawyer or judge in the situation and that you choose to make decisions for yourself.

Listen with Love and Understanding

A good counselor is always a good listener. A good friend can be both counselor and listener to a person moving into a divorce. Most people do not need answers. They need people who will listen to them in love and understanding. And listening takes time and patience. It is hearing people out and letting them vent their feelings, frustrations, and hostilities. It is trying to understand where they are coming from in their life.

You can help a divorcing friend by offering to listen whenever he or she needs it. The first months after the initial separation can be the loneliest and hardest. Good friends who will listen are valuable. And remember that listening with love means refusing to draw judgments.

Be Supportive in Any Way You Can

An old song says it very well: "Just call on me, brother, if you need a hand. We all need somebody to lean on." We have all had the experience of needing help and support from another person in difficult times. Another song proclaims that "no man is an island, no man can stand alone." A divorcing person needs a group of people around who can help in human and practical ways. It may mean helping with a move, having a garage sale, finding a new job, arranging baby-sitting, finding a lawyer, etc. Doing everything alone in post-divorce adjustment can be frightening and emotionally draining. Having a corps of friends who can assist where needed is encouraging. Asking the simple question, "How can I help?" will convey your supportiveness.

Give Direction Where You Can

Advice is cheap. We all have an opinion on everything under the sun. But getting good directions from other people is sometimes very difficult. Giving good directions is even tougher. What we learn by our own experience does not make us an authority on the subject, but it may give us something valuable to pass along to someone else. Know your limitations when giving help and direction to other people. Help where you feel comfortable and where you can.

Refer People to Available Resources

Every community has an endless list of human resources. Most people are totally unaware that they even exist simply because they have never needed them. The first resource that a person going through a divorce needs is a competent lawyer. Other needed resources might be a social worker, a job counselor, and a professional therapist or counselor.

Many people who have gone through a divorce can recommend some very competent assistance to those entering the experience. There are many divorce-recovery workshops that are offered by churches, community colleges, and counseling centers. They may have different names, but all seek to help a person through the entire process of divorce. One of the by-products of this kind of workshop is that you meet and share with other people like yourself. New friendships are made and new growth takes place.

Another unused and overlooked resource is the public library. There are numerous good books that will enlighten and assist the divorcing person. A short bibliography is found at the back of this book.

A divorced person is in the process of making a transition from one way of living to another. It is a difficult process and one that requires a great deal of help and patience. If you have experienced divorce in your own life, you can be a great help to someone else by sharing some of the things in this chapter and some of the things you have personally learned.

Suggestion: Make copies of this chapter and send them to any and all who don't understand what you are going through.

FIFTEEN

Growing Through Divorce...A Summary

You Can Go Through It
or Grow Through It!

This is the thought that we have been sharing with you throughout this book. You can become a battered, bruised, and bitter statistic like so many thousands of divorced persons today, or you can let your divorce be a growth-producing experience in your life. You can use it to build a better you and a better life for you.

We have not intimated anywhere in this book that divorce is an easy process and to be treated lightly. It is a hard, cold, emotion-wrenching experience that can devastate a human being. It is probably one of the least understood and most ignored social problems of our time. Little understanding and less help is available to those caught in divorce.

We have shared in these pages some practical insights and guidelines that can help you turn your divorce into a growth experience. We have offered no easy solutions, no magical cures, no philosophizing. We have said that divorce hurts, and it does. It takes time and hard work to heal the hurts. There will be some days when you will feel so low that you will have to reach up to touch bottom. There will be other days when you will feel that the battle is won. You will have good days and bad days.

I encourage you to put the principles and suggestions from this book into practice in your life. *You have to do the work.* The book will not do it for you.

I want to leave you with these words of hope, written by the apostle Paul to some early struggling Christians: "We are afflicted in every way, but not crushed; perplexed, but not despairing; persecuted, but not forsaken; struck down, but not destroyed" (1 Corinthians 4:8,9).

I would add a further word containing a promise from David the psalmist: "The Lord is close to the brokenhearted and saves those who are crushed in spirit" (Psalm 34:18 NIV).

Working Guide

How to Use This Guide

As the title of my book suggests, I want to help you grow through divorce. I want to help you receive each day as a unique gift, with new lessons to be learned, new healing to be found, and new steps to be taken. As you read through this working guide for chapters 1–10, you'll get to know the person you are—and you'll come to like him or her! You'll have the chance to let God help you grow through divorce, and you'll come to know His tender and healing love. You'll also set goals for yourself, and you'll achieve them. Before we begin, remember to give yourself time. Don't baby yourself, but do be patient with yourself. Growth—of a tomato plant or a tree, of a child or an adult—happens a little at a time. Growth happens a day at a time as we face the decisions, experiences, and hurdles of a given 24-hour period. You grow a little each day, even if you can't see it or feel it. You may not always be able to greet the morning with the exultant words of the psalmist: "This is the day which the Lord has made; we will rejoice and be glad in it" (Psalm 118:24 NKJV), but you can still close the day with thanks to Him for caring about the details of your life, for walking with you as you deal with them, and for promising to be with you tomorrow.

By Yourself

When you pick up this working guide, pick up a pen or pencil as well. This guide is designed for you to *use*, not just to read—and a pen will encourage you to do more than just read the words. Your answer does not need to be long. Don't worry about sentence structure or correct spelling. This is not a test! The working guide is an opportunity for you to think about some issues in your life, to face the emotions which may be hiding inside you, and to get to know yourself a little better. The more thought and effort you put into your answers, the more growth you'll experience.

With a Group

If you are a small-group leader, let this guide to *Growing Through Divorce* be a resource tool as you design your 12-week divorce-recovery workshop. As you plan your weekly meetings, consider the following suggestions.

In your discussion times, emphasize the "Sowing" and "Reaping" sections. The "Sowing" sections are a time of Bible study. The power of God's Word can heal, encourage, challenge, instruct, and comfort. Let that power be released into your group by spending time studying the passages which introduce each lesson. The "Reaping" sections allow a family spirit to develop within your group. People will reach out to one another as they hold each other accountable to goals they set. Friendships will develop as they struggle to reach those goals, as they discuss goals not yet achieved, and as they celebrate goals that they meet.

Let the "Tending" sections be done privately, at least at the beginning of the workshop series. People who are experiencing a divorce are emotionally raw and vulnerable. Be sensitive to this, and don't force your group members to share when they aren't yet ready to. As they get to know each other better, choose questions from the "Tending" sections which you feel are appropriate for group discussion, and include these in your meeting time.

The best guideline I can offer is this: *Be sensitive.* Get to know your group—both the individuals and the personality of the group as a whole. Be aware of the participants' moods, hurts, and questions. Strive to know when and how much to push. Make yourself available on a one-to-one basis. Be able to suggest professional counselors and psychologists for those who are interested.

Pray for the individuals in your group. This guide, the book, and your group are tools which our healing God can use. It is the tool of prayer, however, which will release that power into people's lives like no meeting or book can do by itself.

ONE

Is This Really Happening to Me?

Sowing

"The Lord is close to the brokenhearted and saves those who are crushed in spirit" (Psalm 34:18 NIV).

• Do you feel that God is standing close to you or far away from you right now?

If you are feeling isolated, broken, and discouraged, consider how God can save you from this.

Sometimes He has to save us from ourselves and our self-inflicted wounds. It is easy to blame ourselves when we are down, and lock our spirits inside the prison of self-pity.

At other times, He has to rescue us from those around us who appear to help but in reality hinder. He brings us back to a basic trust in Him alone.

In the last area, God saves us from situations that can damage us further. He moves us into new and safer places.

God does stand close. Can you feel that closeness today?

• Which feeling best describes your situation right now?
  Blame
  Self-pity
  Trust in God

• Even if you can't *feel* God's closeness, *choose* to believe that He is near. Choose to believe His promise to stand by you. Follow up the question, "Is this really happening to me?" with Psalm 34:18; Psalm 46:1; Romans 8:31; or Deuteronomy 31:8.

Tending

Now let's get more in touch with the feelings you may have right now. Put a check mark next to those emotions you are experiencing. This kind of acknowledgment is an important part of being honest with yourself—a point I emphasized in my opening letter to you.

Shocked	Bitter
Vindictive	Angry
Hateful	Betrayed
Dazed	Empty
Numb	Hostile
Cheated	Other:

You probably checked more than one emotion, and such emotional chaos is normal. Repeat this aloud: "Emotions are normal. My emotions are natural." Throughout this guide I'll ask you to say aloud such positive statements. The word "freedom" will be your cue to say the sentence aloud and so declare its truth. The purpose is to reinforce ideas which are affirming, healing, and freeing.

Generally the first stage that divorcing people experience is *shock*. And shock manifests itself in various ways. Which of these things have you found yourself doing?

Retreating into yourself.

Denying what is happening.
Refusing to talk about the divorce.
Withdrawing from friends and social contacts.
Moving to a new home.
Changing jobs.
Struggling with a sense of failure.
Battling an intense feeling of guilt.
Transferring your anger to an innocent party.
Telling everyone who will listen all the details of
    your situation.
Keeping up a frantic social life.
Hiding behind a busy schedule.
Clinging to hope that is based more in fantasy
    than in reality.

If you aren't sure about the wisdom of the hope you're nursing, review the questions on pages 11–13. Remember to be honest with yourself.

Whatever behaviors you placed a check mark by, these behaviors may be fading. The shock may be starting to wear off, and you may find yourself *adjusting* somewhat to your new situation. Shock is accepting the facts of divorce and adjusting is doing something about it. Consider these possibilities.

1. *Positive mourning.* Which of the following statements can you say aloud as an act of self-emancipation?

I'm glad I had the good times, and I wish I still had them.

I'm sorry that the good times are gone now, but I know that there is still much happiness left for me in life.

I have the human right to feel loss, grief, and sorrow.

I hurt, and for now there is an empty space in my life.

2. *Negative mourning.* Which of these statements remind you of yourself?

I feel as if I'm sinking in a sea of self-pity.

I feel that the end of the marriage was all my fault.

I feel that the end of the marriage was all my former spouse's fault.

I feel that life has dealt me a bad hand, and I'm going to let everyone know it.

3. *Assembling the pieces.* How is your life right now like a jigsaw puzzle? What pieces of your life are most difficult for you to work with?
>Sense of disorganization to life
>Extreme emotional highs and lows
>Loneliness
>Being a single parent
>Looking for a job
>Deciding where to live
>Struggling to explain the situation to family (kids included) and friends
>Other:

This time of tending has been a time of evaluation. Since growth happens only when conditions are right, it is important to know what the conditions of your life are. Again, acknowledgment and honesty with yourself provide fertile ground for growth. The crucial step, however, involves making a choice.

Reaping

• Today I could say aloud with a degree of confidence the following statement of positive mourning:

• This week I will carry with me the following idea and so strive to keep my mourning from inhibiting my growth:

• This week I will limit my time for feeling sorry for myself to:
>   30 seconds
>   15 seconds
>   10 seconds

Note that the preceding three instructions involve choices. You can choose one or the other from each of the following pairs:

Hating yourself.

or

Learning to like yourself.

Refusing to believe you'll survive.

or

Believing not that you'll merely survive, but that you'll emerge healthier and stronger than before.

Thinking of divorce as negative and self-defeating.

or
Looking at divorce as an experience
which can help you grow.

Going through divorce.
or
Growing through divorce.

What choices are you making in your life? List one or two from above or from the nine "Growing Through Divorce" steps on pages 17 and 18 of the text as reminders of where you're heading.

1.

2.

Now set a few more goals for yourself. Base them on the "Growing Through Divorce" steps which you just reviewed.

• This week I will meet with a healthy person who is struggling but growing. I will spend time with _____.

• I will take time for myself to think, read, reflect, or meditate. I will spend (how many?)_____quiet moments on (day?)_____ as a time of rest and renewal.

• Daily I will commit my way to God on this new path. I will begin each morning by

—praying.
—reading the Bible.
—quietly listening and thinking.
—all of the above.

• This week I will battle a little with the issue of forgiveness. I will have as my weapon the following fact: People rank sins and tend to make divorce the unforgivable one; God does not rank our sins. Instead, He promises to forgive each and every one that we confess (1 John 1:9).

One more time: Are you choosing to go through or grow through your divorce experience?

FREEDOM: I choose to

P.S.
(This space is for sharing what is on your heart and your mind right now. Your words are confidential. Be a good friend to yourself and talk through whatever is bothering you by writing it on paper.)

Two

Letting Go

Sowing

"Be glad for all God is planning for you. Be patient in trouble, and prayerful always" (Romans 12:12 TLB).

• Would you like God to tell you all He is planning for you in the next year or five years?

• Consider the inevitable struggles which lie ahead. How would knowing about these in advance affect you? Would the results be positive or negative?

God's instruction is simply to be happy for all He is planning for us. He is the Architect of our lives and knows what He is doing. His caution to us as He reveals that daily plan is to be patient when the tough times come, and to always be prayerful. Patience and prayer are the dynamic duo of the Christian walk. Both of them reside near the top of the "tough to do" list in our Christian life.

We do not know how God's plans are going to work out for us today. We do know that we can be glad, because God knows exactly what He is doing. We wait patiently and we pray continually. God reveals the process.

The Architect is at work in your life today. Trust Him!

• What evidence of God's wisdom do you find in the world around you?

• How can this evidence influence your trust in God?

• Paul's instruction to the Roman church is instruction for you today: Be patient and pray. Have you tried doing either of these? The *choice* (there's that word again!) is yours. Let me add that, besides helping you be more patient, prayer will allow you to better know the loving Architect of your life.

By definition, moving forward means moving away from something. That "something" tends to be the known, the familiar, and that "something" therefore involves security. Even if the familiar is unhealthy or painful, it is nevertheless comfortable because there are no surprises or breaks in the routine.

• Do you hesitate to let go of old things and exchange them for something new?

• Are you struggling with fear of the unknown?

Let the next section help you see the unknown that lies ahead as less threatening. Let the next section help you anticipate some of the mental, social, physical, and spiritual changes you may experience as you learn to let go of the past and its pain.

Tending
Having acknowledged either some natural reluctance or some understandable hesitation about the transition from "married" to "single," look more closely at each of the four areas of possible growth.

Mental

What attitudes do the following people *seem* to have toward you? (Let me remind you that you are unable to be objective as you answer this question. You are also unable to be sure that your perception is accurate.) What attitude do you have toward them? Be honest. Let out whatever is inside you, and find yourself letting go of this unhealthy baggage.

	Their Attitude Toward Me	My Attitude Toward Them
Former Spouse		
Children		
Relatives		
Friends		

Often, first attitudes and reactions are not permanent. People's attitudes change; your attitudes change. Repeat this exercise from time to time and see what happens. Some friends will stand by you, some relatives will be less angry as they come to terms with reality, and some of your own feelings will soften.

Social

Where have you noticed (or where do you anticipate) the toughest transition from being married to being single?

Job/career

School/education

Church/religion

Community involvement

Lifestyle

Support system of friends

Be specific. The power of a fear or struggle becomes less once we acknowledge what we are up against.

FREEDOM: I have to face some changes and probably some discrimination in my social life, but none of this is a commentary on my value as a person.

Physical

• At what point during your daily routine do you most notice the absence of your former spouse?

• What can you do to ease the sting of that moment? Be creative! Can you rearrange your routine? Can you call a friend? Can you call on God?

FREEDOM: Being alone right now is not a life sentence imposed as a penalty for my divorce.

Spiritual

• Is your divorce driving you *away from* God or *toward* God?

• If you answered "away from God," consider these things:

—God made you an emotional person. It's okay to be angry—even angry at God.

—Don't confuse your church with God. He is more accepting of us than other people are.

—Don't stay away from God because you feel that your divorce is an unforgivable sin. God doesn't rank sins!

• If you answered "toward God," you have beside you the greatest Caretaker. He will sow seeds of growth and see them through to harvesttime.

FREEDOM: God forgives me even when people around me don't seem able to, and this forgiving God is the Author of new beginnings.

Reaping

This lesson's four statements of freedom were four statements about letting go

— of responsibility for other people's thoughts and feelings.

— of feeling worthless and unable to have healthy relationships.

— of the troubling illusion that you'll be lonely forever.

— of the idea that God cannot or will not forgive you for your divorce.

Now we'll focus on reaching out and replacing those life-draining ways with life-giving goals. First, though, be aware of the choice you're making.

FREEDOM: I am choosing to let go of old things and replace them with new things.

Now say aloud, "I am divorced. I am single. I am OK." How easy was that?

_____

Painless   Difficult

Do this weekly and note your progress as you face reality more directly.

Mental

One positive mental effort this week was

This week I gave (whom?)_____the benefit of the doubt when he/she seemed cold and uncaring.

This week I will remember (write the freedom statement which is most appealing to you right now):

Social

One positive social encounter this week was when

This week I will initiate some social activity by
—striking up a conversation with the boss.
—investigating other career paths.
—talking to a professor/teacher after class about the lecture.
—calling up someone from church whom I've always wanted to get to know better.
—attending a meeting of the local_____(choose a community group).

—being a friend to _____ instead of waiting
for someone to be a friend to me.
—being a good friend to myself by cooking something special or taking myself out to dinner.

Physical

This week, on (day)_____ at (time)_____ I noticed
that the physical absence of my former mate didn't bother me
as much as it once did.

This week I will compensate for the physical absence by

Spiritual

One positive sign of spiritual health from this week was

This week I will try to improve my relationship with God
by

Review the list of "Keys to Accepting a New Identity" on
page 26 and 27 of the text. Now set goals for yourself.

Key 2: This week I will create a "new experience in
living" by

Key 3: At least once this week I will break out my
mold of
—mother/father.
—employee/employer.
—other:

I will do this by

Key 6: This week I will act on my freedom to fail. I will take a risk and try_____. If I fail, I'll learn something from the experience.

FREEDOM: I can let go of the past, grab on to exciting new things today, and so grow toward the future. This process will take time—and I will allow whatever time it takes because I'm worth that investment.

P.S.

THREE

Getting the Former Spouse in Focus

Sowing

"How tremendous is the power available to us who believe in God" (Ephesians 1:19,20 PHILLIPS).

• Do you believe in God?

• Are you tapping into the power that He offers to us as His people?

Knowing God's power is ready for us to claim in all situations gives us the strength to face life's daily conflicts and problems. It does not do us any good, however, if we never use it. It is like being a millionaire and living in poverty. You have to use what is available to you or it will do you no good.

All of God's power is ready for us to plug into: power to live, power to meet frustrations, power to know the right decisions, power to make the necessary changes in our lives that will help us grow.

Are you tapping into God's power in your daily life? Try it today. You will be surprised at the results!

• In what daily situations would you like to experience God's power?

• How are you tapping into that divine power source? Through prayer? Trust? Study? Meditation?

• Choose one hurdle that you are currently facing and ask for God's involvement—for His guidance and His peace as well as His power.

It is quite likely that you listed as a daily situation which could be helped by God's power "dealing with my former spouse." That's the hurdle we'll be looking at in this lesson.

• How do you feel about your former spouse right now?

Hostile	Bitter
Full of pity	Vengeful
Humiliated	Hurt
Betrayed	Other:
Angry	

Tending

Chances are that your feelings toward your former mate are rooted in whatever caused your divorce. Review the list below and look again at pages 29-32 of the text for a description of each cause. Write a brief definition of each type listed.

1. The "Victim" Divorce
2. The "Problem" Divorce
3. The "Little Boy, Little Girl" Divorce
4. The "I Was Conned" Divorce
5. The "Shotgun" Divorce
6. The "Mid-life Crisis" or "Menopause" Divorce
7. The "No Fault" Divorce
8. The "Rat Race" Divorce

Which of the eight causes most closely describes your divorce?

We aren't going to dwell on the reasons or events or circumstances which led to your divorce. While it is wise and necessary to look at some of that (it helps you accept the reality of your situation), too much looking back only prevents growth. We are therefore going to look at five guidelines to help you get your former spouse in a healthier focus—healthier for *you*.

1. Take the detachment one day at a time.

• This is not the first time you've heard this! Is "one day at a time" a wise approach to life? Why or why not?

• Worry removes our focus from the day and from God and instead has us looking toward the future with fear and trembling. Look up Philippians 4:6,7 and write it below as a freedom statement.

FREEDOM:

2. Try to make the break as clean as possible.

• Is a clean break a good idea? Why or why not? (I firmly believe that a clean break is the only healthy way to deal with a divorce. Only a clean break will promote your personal growth. Review pages 36–39 for why I am adamant about this.)

• How clean has your break from your spouse been?
  —We made the break as clean as possible.
  —Our lives are still quite entangled.

• How are your lives still intertwined?
  We share meals.
  We share baby-sitting duties.
  We share gardening/cooking/car-repair chores.
  We share a sexual relationship.
  We share a dating relationship.
  I use every opportunity to see him/her, even though it's never been an entirely positive experience.
  I seem to have forgotten all the bad, and so I nurse the hope that we'll get back together.
  Other:

FREEDOM: I will be happier when I begin to build a new life for myself—and that won't happen as long as I cling to the past.

(What choice is the basis of this freedom?)

3. Quit accepting responsibility for your former spouse.

• Which thoughts have concerned you since your divorce?
  Can my former mate make it on his/her own?
  Will he/she commit suicide?
  What if he starves?
  What if her house and car fall apart?
  What if he/she has a nervous breakdown?
  What if she can't find a job?
  What if he doesn't send the child support?
  Other:

• Are you feeling the desire to take care of your former mate? Is this healthy for you?

• Are you thereby forcing him/her into a state of dependence on you? Is this healthy for him/her? For you?

FREEDOM: Few people learn to stand alone and discover their own resources and abilities *until they have to*.

4. Don't let your children intimidate you.

• How are you feeling because of your children's actions, statements, and attitudes?

Guilty	Empty
Like a failure	Pressured
Bewildered	Heartbroken
Misunderstood	Other:
Frustrated	

• What motives are probably behind the things your children do or say right now? Let this understanding help you be more patient with them and less hard on yourself.

FREEDOM: I acknowledge that children cannot always understand adult decisions.

I love my children and will continue to do so even though their behavior hurts me.

I don't need to be intimidated by my children, especially when I remind myself that their behavior stems from their own hurt, confusion, and insecurity.

5. Don't get trapped in your "child" state.

• Which of the following behaviors have you fallen into since your divorce?

—Throwing temper tantrums.

—Wanting to "get even" with your former spouse.

—Telling lies.

—Being jealous.

—Fighting over petty things.

—Calling your former spouse names.

—Letting the phone ring and then hanging up when he/she answers.

—Spying on your former mate.

—Spreading negative information (whether true or false) among your friends.

Other:

• What does such childish behavior accomplish?

FREEDOM: My growth will happen more easily if my dealings with my former spouse are handled under the conditions of a truce rather than a war.

Reaping

• This week I was pleased about the following aspect of my encounter with my former spouse:

• Which growth guideline seems the easiest for you to work on this week?

• Write out one or two specific goals for yourself which will help you follow that guideline.

1.

2.

FREEDOM: Everyone benefits when people are treated with respect and dignity. I will begin to treat my former spouse in this way. My part of the war is over!

P.S.

Four

Assuming Responsibility for Myself

Sowing

"O Lord God! You have made the heavens and earth by your great power; nothing is too hard for you!" (Jeremiah 32:17 TLB).

• What else in creation reveals to you God's great power?

Jeremiah wrote today's words while he was in prison. He was looking beyond the problems Israel faced to its future. He saw disarray and impending defeat all around him. Yet he called forth the reality that the God who made everything by His power still had enough of that power available to meet daily situations. He affirmed that God could handle His own problems as well as those of Israel.

Do you have two lists of problems in your life? One contains the things *you* will handle, and the other the things you want *God* to handle. I suggest that you make one list today and simply give it to God. Then believe that you can't come up with anything that He is not able to take care of.

• List those problems or concerns which seem too big for you to handle. Then give the list to God.

• List those things which seem too small and insignificant to bother God with. Give these to God as well.

• If there is anything you're concerned about which isn't on either list, make a third list and—you guessed it—give it to God!

As this lesson will point out, assuming responsibility for yourself does not mean tackling life as the Lone Ranger. It doesn't mean being completely self-sufficient and totally independent of God and of the people He puts into your life to help you. "Assuming responsibility for yourself" is simply another way of saying "grow through your divorce." Learn from the experience, learn about yourself, and learn healthful ways to deal with the situations of life.

Tending

• Why is each one of us so ready to blame something or someone else for the circumstances of our life?

• Who are you blaming for your divorce?

Spouse	The office flirt
Job stress	The church
Society's pressures	"We just grew apart"
Children	Parents/in-laws
Neighborhood	Self
Friends' patterns	Other:

Whatever or whomever you find to blame, the fact is that the tendency to blame inhibits your growth. Blaming prevents you from understanding yourself and your situation. What's the alternative? Assuming responsibility for yourself. Let's look closely at five areas for potential growth.

1. I assume responsibility for my part of the failure of my marriage.

• How easy is it for you to say the following statement aloud: "I contributed to the failure of my marriage"?

Simple   Difficult

• Why is such a statement difficult to make—if not for you personally, for other people?

• Do you have standards of perfection for yourself that not even God has for you?

FREEDOM: I have failed in my marriage—but that does not mean that I am a failure, a person destined to fail at everything I try. I can and will move ahead.

2. I assume responsibility for my present situation.

• Wishing things were different accomplishes nothing. Working toward change is the only solution. Complete the following chart. Think carefully and creatively. I've given you cues in the left-hand column.

	I am responsible for:	I will fulfill this responsibility by:
(As an employee)		
(As a parent)		
(As a homeowner/renter)		
(As a breadwinner)		
(As a job-hunter)		
(As a church member)		

FREEDOM: I can do all things through Christ who strengthens me (Philippians 4:13 NKJV).

3. I assume responsibility for my future.

• Since opening this guide, you've had the chance to set positive goals for yourself. Maybe the goals you've set are few in number or still rather undefined. That's OK. Whatever you have is a start. Work toward clarifying your goals, then work toward achieving them. Remember one wise person's words: "Shoot at nothing and that is what you will hit."

• Jot down two or three goals from whatever facet of your life you are most excited about right now. The goals may be mental, social, spiritual, educational, vocational, family-oriented, or designed for personal growth.

FREEDOM: "I will instruct you and teach you in the way you should go; I will guide you with My eye" (Psalm 32:8 NKJV).

4. I assume responsibility for myself—for my thoughts, feelings, and actions.

Thoughts

• We won't dwell on whatever negative thoughts are haunting you. Instead, I want you to consider the source of those thoughts. Where do you think they come from?

Guilt	Anger
Loneliness	Other people's comments to you
Tiredness	An overactive imagination
Laziness	Other:
Fear	

• Do you have to give credibility to the source you just identified? No! In other words, you can choose not to believe that source and those negative thoughts. You can choose to let go of those destructive ideas and replace them with the words of God and the statements of freedom that you'll find in the Bible and in this guide.

FREEDOM: I can control what I think about.

Feelings

• How are you feeling right now? This will be harder for some of you than it is for others—and that's OK.

Angry	Calm
Lonely	Frustrated
Depressed	Lovable
Afraid	Guilty
Hopeful	Trusting
Strong	Other:

• There are several reasons why you may have had a hard time with the previous question. Perhaps you never learned to share your feelings. Maybe you've never been allowed to really be aware of your feelings. Perhaps you've been taught that feelings are bad. Or maybe you're so overwhelmed by a barrage of feelings that you can't distinguish one from another.

FREEDOM: Feelings simply are. Feelings are natural and normal. I am responsible for what I do with my feelings, but I am not responsible for having them.

Action

Hear the words of Paul: "For what I am doing, I do not understand. For what I will to do, that I do not practice; but what I hate, that I do" (Romans 7:15 NKJV).

• Have you ever felt the frustration he expresses?
Yes, often.
Yes, from time to time.
Rarely.
No, not at all.

• Most of us can identify with what Paul says. We act the way we don't want to act. We also *react* in ways we don't want to. Reacting gives another person undeserved and unhealthful control over us. Again a choice is involved—and the choice is yours. Can you repeat the following pledge to yourself? You may find that you have to repeat it frequently—and that's OK!

I choose not to let my former spouse push my buttons. I will act rather than react.

FREEDOM: I can choose to act, not react.

Reaping

• As I think back over the week, I realize that I took responsibility when I

• This week I will assume responsibility for my present situation by

• This week, instead of shooting for nothing, I will assume responsibility for my future by
— clarifying my goals.
— talking to a person who can help me reach a goal (be specific about which goal and which person!).
— spending time alone to get to know my hopes and dreams.

— spending time with God in prayer and study—I want my goals to be His goals for me.
— other:

• This week I will carry the following verse or statement of freedom with me to replace any negative thoughts that come to mind:

• This week I will allow myself to *feel* my feelings. I may even risk sharing them with a friend. _____ would be a good listener I could trust.

• This week I will strive to act in a situation rather than react to it. I will count to ten, for instance, before responding to something my former spouse says.

FREEDOM: Assuming responsibility is not easy. Assuming responsibility takes time. But assuming responsibility is an important part of my own growth—and God will help me through it.

P.S.

FIVE

Assuming Responsibility for My Children

Sowing

"Be kind to each other, tenderhearted, forgiving one another, just as God has forgiven you because you belong to Christ" (Ephesians 4:32 TLB).

• Why should we believers be kind, tenderhearted, and forgiving in our behavior toward one another?

Paul always spoke about the practical things in the Christian life. He did not live in the clouds of biblical doctrine all the time, as some would have us believe. Much of his writing to the early church was highly relational. He wanted the members of God's family to learn how to live with each other in peace and harmony.

The early Christians were just like today's models. They had to be reminded and encouraged repeatedly. Paul did this by constantly reminding them what Christ had done for them. They were "forgiven" and they "belonged." It was this spirit that they were to show to one another.

God's relational glue is comprised of kindness, tenderheartedness (a warm spirit), and forgiveness. God's love gives us these ingredients in great quantities. We are to transmit them to our brothers and sisters in God's family.

• What is one act of kindness that you have done during the past week?

• How can a warm spirit (tenderheartedness) help you live according to Jesus Christ's greatest commandment—to "love the Lord your God with all your heart...and love your neighbor as yourself"?

• How does forgiveness lead to harmony between people?

Kindness, tenderheartedness, and forgiveness help members of God's family live together in peace and harmony. They also help members of your nuclear family live together in peace and harmony because they help you deal with your children during this time of pain and adjustment as you strive to fulfill your God-given responsibility toward them. This lesson will offer you insights and practical suggestions about how to be a parent to your children. Let this lesson also encourage you not to let your children be orphans of your divorce. Parents don't divorce their kids when they divorce each other.

Tending

FREEDOM: Raising children as a single parent is not impossible.

• Which problem common to single parents is most pressing for you right now? If you seem to be surrounded by all four, rank them from greatest (1) to least (4). Read through the points which follow the list.

"My circuits are on overload."

"Where are you when I need you?"
"I don't get any respect."
"Help! I'm a prisoner!"

"My circuits are on overload." Be honest with yourself, with God, with trusted friends, and with people who are in a similar situation. Pent-up frustrations won't stay inside forever, and when they come out they're likely to be directed toward the children you are trying so hard to love.

"Where are you when I need you?" An amicable relationship with the children's other parent will help the two of you be an effective mother and father. Remember this fact when you are tempted to let communication with your former spouse die.

"I don't get any respect." Receiving respect often comes in return for respect that is offered. Are you respectful of your former mate when you speak about him/her in front of the children? Do you respect your children as they deal with their pain and sense of loss in their own way?

"Help! I'm a prisoner!" All of us need to work on keeping our lives in balance. The "how-tos" can be difficult, and they vary from situation to situation. Again, let trusted friends help you gain a more objective perspective of your life.

FREEDOM: I am not the only person ever to struggle with being a single parent—and this struggle is appropriate because the task is difficult!

The following guidelines are designed to help you be an effective single mother or single father. Look closely at each one of them. Applying them to your life will restore some of the joys and rewards of parenting.

1. Don't try to be both parents to your children.

• How have you been trying to be both mother and father to your children?

• How do you feel in this unnatural and impossible role you've defined for yourself?

• Have you tried explaining to your children that you can't be both mother and father to them, but that you will work hard at being the best mother or father you can be? Good communication is as important in a parent/child relationship as it is in any other relationship.

2. Don't force your children into playing the role of the departed parent.

• Have you asked, either verbally or implicitly, your son to be a daddy or your daughter to be a mommy?

• Think about how you feel under the self-imposed pressure to be both mother and father. What similar feelings might your son feel about being forced to be a daddy or your daughter to be a mommy?

• A child needs to be a child! Don't hesitate to give your children new jobs or responsibilities around the house, but don't force them to take on an adult or parental role.

3. Be the parent you are.

• Why is it tempting to be a buddy or pal instead of Mom/Dad?

• Again, put yourself in your child's place. Does he/she need you to be a buddy? Or does he/she need you to continue to be a parent, thereby providing stability and continuity during the turmoil of a divorce?

• A parent—you—needs to be the parent! Don't abdicate that role. Don't escape into a childlike role. That will help no one!

4. Be honest with your children.

• How truthful have you been?
    I've done the best I could.
    I didn't want to hurt them so I fudged a little.
    I told them as much as I thought they could handle.
    I was honest—and it was worth the pain we all felt,
        the pain that now we all share.
    Other:

• How can your honesty be an important gift to your children? See Richard Gardner's perspective on page 59 of the text.

5. Don't put down your former spouse in front of your children.

• Why is it very tempting and quite easy to say negative things about your former spouse?

• What would be accomplished by such talk?

• Let me repeat something from the text: "Most children don't really care who did what to whom. What they care about is what is going to happen to them." Concentrate your energy on reassuring and loving your children rather than on bad-mouthing your former spouse.

6. Don't make your children undercover agents who report on the other parent's current activities.

• How could playing the role of spy for you affect your children's feelings about you?

• Why is it unfair to put a child in the middle between his/her divorcing parents?

• At times it's hard to be an adult, but this time it is a *must*. Don't force your children to play "I Spy" for you.

7. The children of divorce need both a mother and a father.

• Do you have the right to deprive your children of their other parent? Only occasionally—as in an instance of molestation or physical, emotional, and psychological abuse—will the answer be yes.

• How would you feel if your former spouse decided that your children didn't need you?

• Parents are forever. This implies the necessity of a continuing relationship between your children and their other parent and between you and him/her.

8. Don't become an "entertainer parent."

• Why is this an easy trap to fall into?

• List three activities which you can enjoy with your child around your house or apartment. I'll get your brainstorming session started:

Read a book together.
Make homemade ice cream.
Walk to the park.
Write a letter to a grandparent.

• Use your imagination! Better yet, use your children's imaginations. Ask them what they would like to do—and then do it together.

9. Share your dating life and social interests with your child.

• Is this a good idea? Why or why not?

• Have you been honest with your children? Write down their responses to your behavior.

• Be honest with your children, yet let them still be children. They are not spies, "Dear Abby," or counselors. Neither are they the enemy which should be kept in the dark at all costs.

10. Help your children keep the good memories of your past marriage alive.

• Will this project be healthy for your child? Why or why not?

• How can this project be healthy for you?

• Taking away your children's good memories is robbery. It is also an invitation to future bitterness, distrust, and cynicism about marriage. You can choose to keep them free of this unhealthy baggage as they grow.

11. Work out a management-and-existence statement for your children with your former spouse.

• How would this help you in your role as a single parent?

• How would your children benefit?

• The possible benefits seem to far outweigh the negatives involved in the development of this agreement. I would encourage you to take this step for your children's sakes, as well as for your own.

12. If possible, try not to disrupt the many areas in your children's lives that offer them safety and security.

• List some of the different people, activities, or involvements which offer your children a sense of security.

• If moving away from this support system is or has been necessary, which elements can you work together to find at your new home?

• The key concept here is adventure. Changes can be threatening—or they can be exciting doors to new experiences. Choose to help your children regard change as adventure.

13. If your child does not resume normal development and growth in his/her life within a year of the divorce, he/she may need the special care and help of a professional counselor.

• Who can help you watch your children and note the ways they are handling the divorce? Don't hesitate to enlist neighbors, the mothers of your children's friends, and schoolteachers in this task.

• Be prepared. Find out the names of two or three reputable counselors. Talk to people they have worked with and then meet with the counselor yourself.

1.

2.

3.

• We take our children to the dentist for their cavities and to the doctor for the flu. We can likewise take them to counselors or psychologists for any emotional healing they need.

FREEDOM: Being a single parent is a skill to be learned— and I will learn it!

Reaping

In reading through the 13 guidelines, you may have noticed some recurring themes:

• Being a single parent doesn't change a parent's call to be unselfish. If anything, that call is only intensified.

• Being a single parent also involves

— the call to honesty when you yourself may be a victim of dishonesty.

— the call to be fair when your own situation is anything but fair.

— the call to maintain a working relationship with your former spouse, whatever has happened and however he/she is acting now.

— the call to be strong in your role as mother/father despite the temptation to throw your hands up in frustration or despair.

— the call to let your children be children in the midst of the very adult problem of divorce.

• Set some goals for yourself as you accept the challenge and rise to the adventure of this changed parental status:

• I will become a better father/mother by

• I will strive to be honest with my children about what is happening. I will begin by clarifying the details about

• Having looked back on the ideas of guideline 8, this week I will do the following activity with my children:

• This week I will work on keeping my children's good memories of my marriage alive by

— not making negative remarks about their father/mother.
— reminding them of the fun we had when we_____.
— other:

Yes, being a single parent is difficult, but it can be done. And it can be a rewarding and fulfilling experience for you as well as for your children.

FREEDOM: A child can grow through divorce, too.

P.S.

Six

Assuming Responsibility for My Future

Sowing

"What a God he is! How perfect in every way! All his promises prove true. He is a shield for everyone who hides behind him. For who is God except our Lord? Who but he is as a rock?" (Psalm 18:30,31 TLB).

• List the aspects of God's character which the psalmist sings about in this passage.

Have you ever run out of superlatives when describing your best friend to someone? You want that person to know how you feel about your friend and what he means to you. David felt that way about God. Although he had his struggles with God, he still affirmed Him to other people.

David tells us in this passage that God is five different things. As we look at them, ask yourself if you could describe God to your friends in these terms.

First, God is perfect in every way. That is difficult for us to grasp because our world is filled with imperfections.

Second, we are told that God stands behind His promises. They are true. When God says something, He does it.

Third, God provides a shield for us to hide behind. When the world throws its heavy artillery at us, we need to shield ourselves while we regroup. God provides a secure hiding place for us when we need it.

Fourth, He is our Lord. That's personal, not general. We belong to Him and He belongs to us.

Finally, He is a rock. For me, that represents stability. He doesn't change game plans and agendas from day to day. He is solid and He is there for me—today and tomorrow.

• Which of these five truths about God do you have the hardest time believing?

• Has God ever given you reason to doubt the perfection of His ways, His faithfulness to His promises, His personal Lordship of your life, or the stability of His plans for you? Don't attribute the behavior and free choices of imperfect and sinful people to the all-loving God! But do talk to God about where your faith in Him may be weak right now. Call on Him to help your unbelief (Mark 9:24).

• Which of the five truths about God offers you hope for the future?

As this lesson will emphasize, each of us needs to assume responsibility for the future, but that doesn't mean going it alone. We need to make decisions and take steps, but we can and should do this with the guidance of our perfect, steadfast, protective, personal, and stable God. Claim the truth of this personality profile and step into the future—step into tomorrow—with confidence and eager anticipation of what it holds for you. God *will* be with you!

Tending

FREEDOM: It's normal for me to feel unenthusiastic, skeptical, or hopeless about the future.

• Whether or not you completed the exercise on page 68 of the text, take the time now to list ten things you are looking forward to in the next several days and weeks. Let your imagination go free. Are you looking forward to a friend's birthday celebration? A long-awaited letter? Learning something new at work? Experimenting with your wok? Taking the risk of making a new friend?

1.

2.

3.

4.

5.

6.

7.

8.

9.

10.

• If you had a difficult time listing ten things, learn something about yourself from that fact.

I learned that

• You might also learn something about yourself from this observation:

I've noticed three kinds of people: those who watch things happen, those who make things happen, and those who don't know what's happening.

If you have goals for yourself, you are probably a person who makes things happen. If you aren't sure this description fits you right now, you can work toward that goal—but your cocoon will have to go! You will be letting go of that cocoon when you make plans for the future and then follow them.

FREEDOM: I am free to fail.

We are all human. We all therefore make mistakes and all experience failure. The healthy way to deal with this inevitable failure is to learn something from the experience and then move forward. Such movement can sometimes be difficult, and then it's both wise and helpful to consult with a trusted friend or respected counselor. These people can help us set realistic goals for ourselves. The following five guidelines are also helpful.

1. Evaluate your present situation.

    • Evaluate your current financial situation. Establish a workable budget.

      What are your monthly expenses?

      What is your monthly income?

      Can some expenses be reduced, if not completely eliminated?

      What options do you have for increasing your income?

      Will the steps toward an increased income call for any extra expenses, whether temporary or ongoing?

    • Look at your job situation.

      Are you working now?

If so, are you satisfied?

If so, what are you working toward in your job?

If you aren't employed, where can you go for assistance?

If you aren't employed, what can you do to rebuild your sense of self-confidence and self-esteem? Try the Bible! Also try low pressure projects which will give you the feeling of having accomplished something.

• Consider your career path.

This is the same question you've been asked all your life: "What do you want to be when you grow up?" Let the sky be the limit as you answer the question. If nothing were impossible, where would you like to be in five years? In ten years?

• This three-part evaluation is the starting point for making plans. The following verse is added incentive.

FREEDOM: "I will instruct you and teach you in the way you should go; I will guide you with My eye" (Psalm 32:8 NKJV)

2. Explore new and potential situations.

• How do you feel about the future? About changes? About the new and the unknown?

• You don't need to be bullied by feelings of fear, a lack of hope, or a sense of discouragement. Instead, choose to see the future as an adventure. You can choose also to see this adventure as being held in the hands of a loving God.

FREEDOM: I choose to be an explorer and adventurer in my approach to the future.

I choose to follow God along this path. (See Psalm 119:105 and Jeremiah 29:11.)

3. Establish short-term and long-term goals.

• Why is it important to establish long-term goals?

• Why is it important and helpful to establish short-term goals as well? How can they serve as stepping-stones toward your long-range plans?

4. Don't be afraid of commitments.

• Are you afraid of commitments right now?

____Yes, terrified!   ____No, not at all.

• Some fear of commitment—some hesitation to be vulnerable—is understandable and quite appropriate for someone experiencing a divorce. Let me remind you, though, that one broken commitment doesn't mean that every future commitment will be broken. A past failure doesn't mean only failure in the future, especially when we take the time to learn from the past. Think carefully about the following things and respond as specifically as you can.

Since your divorce, what have you learned about
— your feelings?
— your ability to deal with new situations?
— the way you cope with pain?
— friendship?
— forgiveness?
— the role of communication in a relationship?
— the importance of honesty?
— your expectations for a marriage relationship?
— your standards for yourself?
— God?

• Read through the Ten Commandments (pages 74-75) for other insights about the past, ways to cope with the present, and ideas to carry you into the future. Rewrite each commandment in your own words so that it speaks specifically to your current situation.

5. Trust God with your future.

• What does the phrase "trust God" mean to you as it is used in this context?

• How can trusting God be active rather than passive? In other words, how is trusting God different from merely waiting for Him to act?

FREEDOM: "Trust in the Lord with all your heart, and lean not on your own understanding; in all your ways acknowledge Him, and He shall direct your paths" (Proverbs 3:5,6 NKJV).

Reaping

• This week I will take a risk. Knowing that it is OK to fail, I will risk

• I will seek to improve my present job situation by
— outlining the progress I've made since coming to work and determining the prospects for the future.
— gathering information about the company's organizational structure, its advancement policies, and its history of promotions.
— talking to the boss about advancement possibilities.
— investigating similar opportunities with different companies.
— other:

• I will consider the career path I'm on and alternatives that might be better in the long run. I will

— brainstorm with a friend about possible options.
— set aside 30 minutes for daydreaming: "If I could do/be anything, I would _____."
— visit a local college's career planning center and familiarize myself with that resource.
— talk to _____, a person who holds a position I only fantasize about right now.
— other: _____.

• Choose one or two long-term goals from the beginning of the "Tending" section. Below, define two or three short-term goals which can help you achieve the grander ones—and then begin to tackle a few of those short-term goals this week.

Long-term Goal Number One:

Short-term goals:

a.

b.

c.

Long-term Goal Number Two:

Short-term goals:

a.

b.

c.

• I will work on improving my level of trust in God by getting to know Him better. To do this, I will

— attend a worship service.

— spend five minutes a day reading the Bible.

— start each day with two or three minutes of prayer.

— close each day with a prayer of thanksgiving for what happened that day.

— set aside ten minutes to be quiet with God.

— pray with a friend.

— other:

P.S.

Seven

Finding a Family

Sowing

"He has given you Paul and Apollos and Peter as your helpers. He has given you the whole world to use, and life and even death are your servants" (1 Corinthians 3:22 TLB).

• Who has God given you—either someone in the past or someone involved in your life right now—as your "helper"?

How would you like to have Paul, Apollos, and Peter as your personal friends and helpers? They certainly were a dynamic trio. With friends like that, you would be a lot stronger in the faith and more courageous in your walk.

Somehow, the Corinthian believers did not realize the value of this trio. They probably did just what you and I do with our good friends—take them for granted. We seldom realize how important friends are to us until they move to another town.

Whom has God given you as friends and helpers in your life? The good friends we have are not there by accident. I believe that God has a way of bringing people into our lives to support us and care for us. Sometimes we move through life so fast that we don't allow people time to connect to us and become God's blessing in our lives.

Are you open to God bringing new friends and helpers into your life today? The next person you meet may be by divine direction. Keep your heart open. He may need you just as much as you need him!

• Write down the names of two or three friends who have helped you be strong in your faith and more courageous in the face of life's hurdles. Be specific about what you appreciate about each of these people.

• Have you taken such good friends for granted? Thank God right now for bringing them into your life. I also encourage you to pick up the phone or a piece of paper and a pen. Let these people know that you appreciate them!

• Having thought about the way God has already blessed you with friends, consider how open you are right now about meeting other people He wants to bring into your life.

— I am open to the blessings of new friends which God wants to give me.
— I want friends and helpers, but right now I'm nervous about taking the risk of getting to know someone.
— I want new friends, but the risk of being vulnerable and possibly being hurt outweighs any benefits that might come with finding a new friend.
— I'm not ready to risk getting close to another person.

• Whatever your answer above, read again the last three sentences of this lesson's devotional. Have you thought of someone needing you as much as—if not more than—you need him or her?

Developing a friendship can be risky business. I have found my church involvement to be a safe place for taking this kind of risk. I have found support and encouragement in God's family—the family we will look at closely in this lesson.

Tending

- First, consider the family you were born into.

  — How did your family receive you?
  — How did you receive them?
  — What did they do for you?
  — What did you do for them?

- Now how is this family reacting to you and your divorce?

- If you are disappointed or hurt by their reactions, try to understand that they may not understand the pain you feel, how to help, or what to say, and that they aren't responsible for the divorce or their own mixed emotions. And if you feel alone right now because of their inability to help, claim this promise:

FREEDOM: "God is our refuge and strength, a very present help in trouble" (Psalm 46:1 NKJV).

- Look for a moment at the family that you married into.
  — What dreams did you have (or do you still have) for this family?
  — Do you still feel a part of this family?
  — How are these people reacting to you and your divorce?

- If you are disappointed or hurt by their reaction, again try to understand that they are struggling with their own confusion, hurt, shock, disappointment, and loyalty to their own son or daughter.

- If you are feeling estranged from your natural family and from your former spouse's family, let me encourage you to discover or rediscover the family of God. When we, God's children, bear one another's burdens, we fulfill the law which our heavenly Father has given us and we build a family which reflects the tender love and constant support which God offers each one of us (see Galatians 6:2). Consider these facts about God's family.

— God's family is a "forever family."
— You join God's family by receiving His Son, Jesus Christ, and recognizing Him as the new Director of your life.
— Membership in this family means growth every day, and that growth comes from study, worship, prayer, and talking with other family members.
— The family of God—huge and enduring as it is—provides its members a sense of belonging that nothing else can.
— Members of God's family have responsibilities to each other as we help each other live according to Jesus' instructions.
— We can't lose our membership in the family of God: "All that the Father gives Me will come to Me, and the one who comes to Me I will by no means cast out" (John 6:37 NKJV).

• What is most appealing about this description of God's "forever family"? In other words, what would you most like to find in this family?

• Write out the following instructions for living in God's family. At the end you'll have a description of the kind of community that God wants us to share with each other.

— Ephesians 4:1-3
— 1 Corinthians 10:24
— Hebrews 12:14,15
— 1 Thessalonians 5:14,15

Reaping

• What will improve your relationship with members of your family? Check whatever answers are appropriate.

Your forgiveness of them
Their forgiveness of you
Time
Patience
Prayer
Swallowing your pride
Dropping your defensive stance
Open, honest, and sensitive communication
God's healing power
Other:

• Turn one of your choices into a goal:

This week I will take a step toward improving my relationship with my family by

• What might improve your relationship with your former spouse's family? Consider some of the elements on the previous list.

• Take time to consider whether pursuing a relationship with your former in-laws is a wise or worthwhile move at this time. If after careful thought and prayer you feel that it is, set yourself a goal for taking a positive step this week. If you don't believe that it is wise to take such a step now, set yourself the goal of praying regularly about the hurt on both sides of the break.

• What local part of God's family would you like to become more involved with? List three or four possibilities here.

• Now set yourself a goal: This week I will call about (which group?)_____ and find out about it. I will ask if any members come from my neighborhood, and if so I will contact him/her about going to the meeting together.

• If becoming involved in God's family means that you first need to become His son or daughter, pray this simple prayer:

God, thank You for the invitation to be part of Your family. Thank You for sending Your Son, Jesus Christ, to die for my sins so that I can become Your son/daughter. Teach me to trust You with my life. Help me to love people more. Train me to follow You more closely. In Your Son's name. Amen.

FREEDOM: "Behold what manner of love the Father has bestowed on us, that we should be called children of God!" (1 John 3:1 NKJV).

P.S.

EIGHT

Finding and Experiencing Forgiveness

Sowing

"If we confess our sins, He is faithful and righteous to forgive us our sins and to cleanse us from all unrighteousness" (1 John 1:9 NASB).

• What does this verse teach about the kind of God our heavenly Father is?

Have you ever struggled with admitting you were wrong in a certain situation or discussion? Remember how hard it was? Wouldn't it be great to always be right and never have to confess that you were wrong?

God created us to be very human. Along with our humanness comes the conflict of right and wrong. God seemed to know that we would make mistakes, so He provided a way to help us take care of them. His formula is, "Confession equals cleansing and forgiveness." It's not an easy formula to live with, but it is the only one that helps us keep a right relationship with both God and man.

Perhaps you have noticed that this promise begins with an *if*. That might prompt you to ask what happens if we don't confess wrongs or sins. From my experience, lack of confession leads to the guilt trap, the anger syndrome, and the pits of depression.

Many of us cart around things that need to be confessed to God. Only when we confess them, admit them, and own up to them can God do anything with them. His promise becomes a cleansing therapy that will keep us whole.

• Why isn't forgiveness "an easy formula" for you to live with?

• Have you experienced the guilt, anger, and/or depression which come when we don't confess our sin? Which of these three feelings do you struggle with most?

• What feelings have you experienced when you've talked to God about a time you were wrong, a mistake you made, an incident when you hurt someone, or your failure to walk closely with Him?

In this lesson we'll deal with the issue of forgiveness as it pertains to your divorce. Whatever the details of your particular situation (you may feel like the innocent victim or you may realize the pain you have caused others), you must come to a point of forgiveness, and that will involve forgiving yourself and forgiving others as well as accepting God's forgiveness.

Tending

Seeds of forgiveness can be cultivated in five areas of your life, and we will look at each one of them.

1. God forgives me!

• For what attitudes and actions—especially surrounding your divorce—do you need to receive God's forgiveness? Be honest with yourself and with God. Let go of the unnecessary baggage of guilt and self-hatred. You can do this only when you acknowledge your failure to live up to God's ideal for marriage and when you recognize the other errors which surrounded your divorce.

• Read again the simple prayer on page 92. This short talk with God can mark a new beginning in your life.

• Read John 8:3-11. Write verse 11 below, and personalize it. Include your name. Hear Jesus speaking those words to you.

FREEDOM: Write the verse which opened this lesson, and write it so that it speaks directly to you.

2. I forgive me!

• Which is harder for you: accepting God's forgiveness or forgiving yourself?

• For what actions or attitudes are you struggling to forgive yourself? Be as specific as possible. This will help you let go of the burden of guilt and the habit of self-flagellation.

• Review the definitions of forgiving yourself that I list on page 93. List below those statements which are, for you, a declaration of independence.

FREEDOM:

• Consider also this statement of freedom from God's Word:

FREEDOM: "But God demonstrates His own love toward us, in that while we were still sinners, Christ died for us" (Romans 5:8 NKJV).

• Remember this verse when you are less forgiving of yourself than your loving God is.

3. I forgive my former spouse.

• Forgiving your former spouse will take time. It will also take a conscious decision on your part as you choose to forgive him or her. When you forgive your former spouse, however, you are actually freeing yourself from a burden of hatred and resentment. You are freeing yourself from thoughts about that person which would continue to control your emotions, if not your actions as well. Forgiveness, though, does not need to involve the potentially condescending pronouncement to the other party, "I forgive you."

• Consider Jesus' instructions about forgiveness and Paul's echo of this teaching. Write the following verses below:
Matthew 6:14,15
Colossians 3:13
Ephesians 4:32

• Spend some time talking to God about your struggle to forgive your former spouse.

4. My former spouse forgives me.

• Receiving the forgiveness of your former spouse may mean asking for that forgiveness. Such asking must be done without a condescending, "holier-than-thou" attitude.

— Examine your motives.

— Ask God to guide you as to what to say and when to talk to your former mate.

— Understand that asking for forgiveness involves admitting your weaknesses and your contributions to the divorce.

• Which of the following responses do you expect?

Gracious acceptance of your request and a statement of forgiveness.

Laughter.

Hostile rejection.

Being ignored.

No response at all.

Other:

• Anticipating the possible response may help you deal with the real-life situation. Consider, though, whether the response of your former mate really has any bearing on your request for forgiveness. Would his/her rejection of you when you ask for forgiveness invalidate your act of repentance? The answer, in case there is any doubt, is *no*! When you acknowledge your responsibility for your divorce and when you approach your former spouse, you have fulfilled your responsibility. You are free to go forward from here.

5. I will forgive and forget.

• Forgetting comes with time. As God heals you, forgetting will be part of the process. And as I alluded to earlier, forgiveness takes time. It is an ongoing process which the God who forgave you will help you through.

• Reread the poem "Prayer for the Divorced" on pages 95-96. Which lines touched you? What message does the poem have for you?

Reaping

• In which of the five areas of your life would you like to experience forgiveness?

• Set goals for yourself in each of the five areas. If you have already experienced forgiveness, thank God for that!

— God's forgiveness
— Forgiveness of yourself
— Forgiving your former spouse
— Receiving forgiveness from your former spouse
— Forgetting

FREEDOM: "As far as the east is from the west, So far has He removed our transgressions from us" (Psalm 103:12 NKJV).

P.S.

◆

NINE

47 Going on 17

Sowing

"There is no fear in love; but perfect love casts out fear, because fear involves punishment, and the one who fears is not perfected in love" (1 John 4:18).

• When has your love for someone cast out the fear that he or she was feeling about something? Think of young children, for instance, or a friend who was facing a hurdle you had once cleared in your own life. Jot down a few details about that situation.

Have you ever made a list of all your fears? It could run all the way from your fear of getting a speeding ticket to cracking your dentures on peanut brittle. The problem with fears is that they seldom become realities. They are ghosts that hide in the closets of our minds, and only come out when we aren't looking. John was aware that even Christians have fears. He knew that fear could prevent the people of God from living a fulfilled life. He knew that only one thing could eliminate fear from the life of the Christian. That one thing was knowing that God's love was stronger in a believer's life than all the fears he could conjure up.

Have you ever tried to give your fears a dose of love? A common fear is the fear of what will happen tomorrow. How do you deal with that fear?

The Scriptures tell me that God is in charge of tomorrow. If I believe that He loves me enough to take me through tomorrow, then there is nothing about it I need to fear. His love will penetrate that fear and remove it from my life.

• What fears are haunting you right now? Don't dwell on this question, but do list three or four things that readily come to mind.

• In his Gospel, John teaches about the love of God:

"For God so loved the world that He gave His only begotten Son, that whoever believes in Him should not perish but have everlasting life" (John 3:16 NKJV).

What bearing does this fact have on the fears you just listed?

• Look up these other words about God's love for you and me. Let their truth replace the fears of your life.
— Romans 5:8
— 1 John 4:7-9
— Romans 8:38,39

Perhaps a fear you listed was fear of the future. One aspect of that perfectly understandable feeling may be your nervousness about once again entering the dating scene. This lesson will focus on the challenging and frustrating, yet potentially quite rewarding, adventure of dating again.

Tending

• In the text I claim that it is a mistake to jump into any kind of relationship until you have had time to adjust to your divorce and to the new demands it has placed on you. Do you agree? Why or why not? As you consider my claim, jot down some of the pros and cons of giving yourself time to heal and adjust.

• Read through the list of fears which are common to people coming out of a divorce. Indicate with a check mark your greatest fear.

Can I be sure that the relationship will last this time?
Can I ever trust another man/woman again?
Will I make the same mistakes again?
Can I be happy if I marry again?
What if I don't find someone?
Will I feel confident and sure enough to begin dating?
Other (or a combination of two or more listed):

FREEDOM: Healing takes time. Learning to trust takes time. My time line is unique to me.

• The questions above point out a choice you can make between the risk of reaching out and the risk of regret. You may reach out and be hurt again, or you may choose never again to be vulnerable and thereby sentence yourself to an isolated existence which will very likely take you to a point of emptiness and regret for opportunities not taken and friendships missed. If you do reach out and if you are hurt, you will survive. God will be with you. Your church family and close friends will stand by you. What choice—whether consciously or by default—are you making right now?

FREEDOM: I choose to

• The fears we just looked at are not helpful if they immobilize us. They are helpful, though, when they caution us to think about the step we're taking into a relationship. Answer these questions for yourself.

What have I learned about myself through my divorce? A corollary question is, Have I taken enough time to learn about my strengths and weaknesses, my typical behaviors in a relationship, and my ability to communicate?

Has enough time elapsed to let the dust settle?
Yes
No
I'm not sure

There is no magic length of time for every person. Healing happens in different ways for each of us. Be sensitive to how much you've healed. Be patient with yourself. You'll then be able to enter a new friendship as a stronger person.

Am I building healthy relationships?

Begin to answer this question by first considering with whom you are building relationships right now. Are they people who are growing? Or are they too close to their own divorce and pain? Is there a balance between giving and receiving in these relationships? What are you giving? What are you receiving?

How much of my past marriage am I dragging into my new relationship?

We are all products of our own experiences; that fact cannot be changed. Still, we need not carry excess baggage with us as we journey through life. Are you still talking about your marriage? Is it hard for you to leave behind that part of your past? If so, you may want to give yourself a little more time before you enter a new relationship.

• Having dealt with your fears and carefully thought about the four points of caution, consider now the issue of trust.

With my trust in God and with His help, I can begin again.

• Do you trust God? Write your own freedom statement. Choose a verse from the Bible or an idea from my discussion of this topic.

FREEDOM: With the help of God, I can learn to love and trust in new ways.

• How can God be a part of your learning process?

• How can a good friend *of the same sex* help you learn to trust?

I will trust that God is doing a new work in my life and will continue to do it.

If and when I remarry, it will be the richest experience of my life.

• Is it easier for you to trust God or other people? Why?

• How can trust in God help you trust other people?

• Write your own statement of trust. How easy is it for you to trust God right now? Be honest with yourself and with Him!

• Write Romans 8:28 below and let that verse help you trust God more.

FREEDOM:

Reaping

• Which fear would you like to put to rest in the next several weeks?

• Develop a goal that will help you do this. The goal can involve choosing again and again not to let the fear control you. The goal can involve taking a small risk of sharing your ideas, feelings, or dreams. The goal can involve turning to God for His healing, His guidance, and His support.

This week I will

• Which caution spoke directly to you and your current situation?

• Write out a caution to carry with you this week. The caution may be a prayer or a reminder of a lesson you've learned the hard way.

• In which current relationship can you risk sharing a little more of yourself? This will be a step of learning to trust more—and you have a lot to gain by taking that step!

Before adding your P.S., spend some time jotting down your ideas about the following excerpt from the text: "Describe the person you married the first time and the kind of person you would like to marry in the future." This valuable exercise will help you understand your fears, follow words of caution, and sow seeds of the ability to trust.

P.S.

TEN

Remarriage—Yours, Mine, and Maybe Our Families

Sowing

"My God shall supply all your needs according to His riches in glory in Christ Jesus" (Philippians 4:19).

• What are some of your daily needs?

Have you ever planned and plotted to get some desired item? You just knew you couldn't live without it. Then, after you acquired it, it sat around and you hardly ever used it. That's why we have so many garage sales in our country. We have garages full of things we had to have but seldom use.

There is a vast difference between what we want and what we need in life. Our want list is usually taken from the merchandisers who really want our money for their products. Our need list is more geared to what we really need to keep alive and well.

On the nonmaterial side, we need love, affirmation, friendship, meaning, and purpose in our lives. And that's just a small part of the list of intangibles.

Paul tells us that God promises to meet each of us on the "need" level of our lives. God's riches are so vast that He can just tap into His inexhaustible supply and distribute them freely to us.

Have you been moping recently over the things you don't have instead of thanking God for what you do have? God always knows what will be good for us, and those are the things He sends our way. God is in the business of meeting our needs—even the most gigantic ones. Trust Him today for yours!

• Look again at your list. Did some "wants" creep into your "needs" list? Cross those off.

• Having read today's devotional, do you want to add any items to your list?

• Circle those items which God is providing for you right now.

• Let me ask you again this important question: "Have you been moping recently over the things you don't have instead of thanking God for what you do have?"

Trust God to meet your needs. Trust Him to know what is good for you and when it is good for you to receive it. Trust Him also to help you be a responsible steward of those things and people with which He does bless you. If, for instance, God seems to be leading you to remarriage with its joys and struggles, its new beginnings and new challenges, seek God's guidance and learn from this lesson.

Tending
This tending should be done by both you and the person you may marry!

• What feelings surface when you hear the word "remarriage"?

panic	skepticism
fear	enthusiasm
wariness	sense of wholeness
longing	hope
caution	impatience
hostility	other:

• Are you at peace with God about this decision to remarry? Honest introspection and sincere seeking after God's will are crucial steps in this decision-making process.

• The decision to marry must be made not only with your heart but also with your mind. Think through the following issues if you are considering remarriage. The nuts and bolts of everyday living call for careful thought rather than just warm feelings. Waiting until these situations occur will not help your new marriage start off strongly.

— How many children are involved? Who will support them?
— Where will they live?
— Will some of your income have to go toward the support of a former spouse and children?
— Where will you live? An old house has ghosts and memories which can haunt a new marriage.
— How will the children address their new parents?
— If your new mate is a noncustodial parent, where will his/her children stay when they visit you?
— Will you be having to deal with legal adoptions and name changes for the children once you marry?

— How will you and your new mate handle the discipline of each other's children?

Now that you're warmed up, think about the following six areas of possible conflict. They involve either an ongoing relationship with a former spouse, the fair treatment of children, or the finances of remarriage—three issues which will never seem to be totally resolved.

• To whom should you be loyal? First list your options. Then rank them, letting number 1 stand for the person who deserves the greatest loyalty from you.

• Now read through my discussion on page 110 of the text. Do these hypothetical situations call into question the ranking you just did? Real life has a way of changing seemingly black-and-white issues into varying shades of gray.

• You may be wondering how you can win with stepchildren. What do you fear about the prospect of dealing with stepchildren?

• Imagine being one of the children. How would you want to be treated? In answering this question, you may provide yourself with some very effective guidelines for your role as a stepparent.

• How can you make stepchildren feel as important as your natural children? Brainstorm about this and the preceding question with your potential spouse.

FREEDOM: I am going to just be myself. Then I can work to become the best stepmother/stepfather I can be.

• What adjustments will you have to make in your lifestyle when the two families become one? To answer this, first describe the two different life styles. Will there be a significant difference between the weekdays and the weekends? Or does the new challenge involve blending your ways with your future spouse? How are the kids caught in the middle? What sacrifices are you being called to make as you adjust to your new situation? Again, jot down ideas, but then be sure to discuss these issues with your potential mate.

• How are you to treat your spouse's former mate?

— How much contact do you anticipate?
— Are you able to be compassionate as you consider the former spouse's situation?
— How amicable was the divorce settlement?
— How might your new marriage help you deal with your former mate?

Again, think about these things and jot down ideas, but also plan to talk a lot with your future spouse about dealings with your exmates.

• How will you be related to new in-laws, former in-laws, and other friends? List the names of people who will be affected by your remarriage and note beside each name the reaction you have received or the reaction you expect.

• Another topic for thought and discussion is how you will deal with these relationships. For which ones will you fight? Which ones will be dissolved? How will you deal with the pain?

• How will you and your mate grow together in your marriage? Write down specific plans you have for making sure that you have time for each other, time to communicate, time to play together, time to work together, and time to worship God together.

Reaping

As with any growing thing, a remarriage does not take root immediately and bloom overnight. But careful and patient cultivation of the relationship will bring satisfaction and fulfillment that is well worth the wait. Such cultivation must be planned.

• This week my future mate and I will meet together (when?) _____ (where?)_____ to discuss
    —children.
    —dealings with former spouse(s).
    —finances.

We will talk about our different lifestyles by comparing the profiles we sketched in the "Tending" section.

    Date
    Time
    Place

• Plan for a time to talk about these issues as well:

— What fears do you have about remarriage?

— What role will God play in your life? In your mate's life? in your life together?

— How important is communicating? How can you keep communication open and vital?

— Consider situations which could arise that would call into question your loyalty to each other. Talk them through carefully now, before the situation is a reality and emotions are at a fever pitch.

— How threatened is each of you by the other's former spouse? By the other's natural children?

• Define two goals for yourself that will help you prepare for your marriage. Consider those habits, attitudes, or behaviors which you would like to be free of, and plan a way to change and grow.

P.S.

Final Review

It is hard for any of us to realize or measure our own growth and recognize the healing that takes place in our lives. We are often too close to our crises (we live with the pain and questions) to be able to see our progress. When we take a moment to look back, we can clearly see the struggling times we have gone through, the new friendships we have made, the steps we took, and the emotions we processed. We move forward through our hopelessness to a renewed hope. Our journey takes on the similarity of the changing seasons of each calendar year.

Author Robert Veninga captures our journey through struggles and joys in these words:

Human pain does not let go of its grip at one point in time....There is a season of sadness, a season of anger, a season of tranquility, a season of hope. But seasons do not follow each other in a lockstep manner....The winters and springs of one's life are all jumbled together in a puzzling array....But when one affirms that the spring thaw will arrive, the winter winds seem to lose some of their punch.

You have spent some long hours within the pages of this book and study guide. It hasn't been fun reading, and you may have set it aside many times because you did not want to face the journey ahead. If you have gotten to this page by reading, processing, and working on your divorce, you will be the better for the experience.

Much healing still lies ahead. The scars from your divorce will remain with you for the rest of your life. Healing will make those scars less noticeable and they will eventually become badges of growth in your life. But always remember, healing takes time and comes from God. This is spoken about in Matthew 8:18 (NIV) when the Gospel writer says, Jesus "healed all the sick. This was to fulfill what was spoken by the prophet Isaiah: 'He took up our infirmities and carried our diseases.'"

Some of our healing occurs when we are alone, while the remainder takes place when we are with other people. Author Henri Nouwen says,

A Christian community is therefore a healing community not because wounds and pains are alleviated, but because wounds and pains become openings or occasions for a new vision. Mutual confession then becomes a mutual deepening of hope and sharing weakness becomes a reminder to one and all of the coming strength.

You need to be on your own track for growth and healing, but you also need a strong Christian support system around you. Remember, you are not the Lone Ranger!

As a final summary to your reading and study of this book, take a few minutes today and respond to the following wrap-up questions.

1. Before I started reading this book I was...

2. Since reading this book I have...

3. As I look ahead now in my life, I will...

4. The things that have helped me the most in this book are...

5. With God's help, as I rebuild my life, I will...

6. Thank you, Lord, for...

And remember the promise from Psalm 34:18 (NIV): "The Lord is close to the brokenhearted and saves those who are crushed in spirit."

SHALOM!

To contact Jim Smoke, please write
to him via e-mail:

jsmoke1745@aol.com

or send a letter to:

Jim Smoke
c/o Harvest House Publishers
990 Owen Loop North
Eugene, OR 97402-9197